Dept ~~~~~~~~~~~~~ ndary
and Technological
Education   Acker

                   HIED

UNDP Policy Discussion Papers

The United Nations Development Programme is the world's largest grant development co-operation organization. It serves as the central planning, funding and co-ordinating agency for technical co-operation by the entire United Nations system. UNDP and its associated funds provide assistance in agriculture, education, employment, fisheries, health, industry, science and technology, transport and communications, and other sectors.

Policy Discussion Papers are part of a research programme recently established by UNDP. The overall objective of the programme is to provide decision makers within UNDP with a rational base for formulating policies and strategies on the organization's future role. The establishment of such a knowledge base, drawing on UNDP's extensive global experience with development, is a crucial step for UNDP in assisting developing countries in a more effective manner, particularly by improving technical co-operation programmes and projects.

More specifically, the discussion papers are intended to provide UNDP staff members and managers with syntheses and analyses of major development policy and technical co-operation issues. By stimulating discussion both within and outside of UNDP, the papers are expected to help identify possible alternative solutions to emerging problems long before these reach crisis proportions. They will also contribute to the establishment of practical UNDP policies and procedures of technical co-operation.

It is hoped that these discussion papers, written by UNDP staff members and outside consultants, research institutes and universities commissioned by UNDP, will act as a spring-board for constructive criticism and suggestions by both scholars and practitioners about how to enhance the effectiveness of current development and technical co-operation programmes and projects.

Education and Training in the 1990s

Education and Training in the 1990s

Developing Countries' Needs and Strategies

Education Development Center

UNDP Policy Discussion Paper

United Nations Development Programme
New York

Copyright © 1989 United Nations
All rights reserved
Manufactured in the United States of America

The opinions expressed in this report do not
necessarily reflect the views or policies of
the United Nations Development Programme

United Nations Publications
Sales No. E.89.III.B.7

ISBN 92-1-126016-7
001900

Contents

Acknowledgements 9
Introduction 11

1. Education 15
   1.1 Issues for the 1990s 16
   1.2 Meeting the Challenges: Promising Approaches for the 1990s 24
   1.3 Undertaking Initiatives to Improve Educational Efficiency 27
   1.4 Improving the Policy Planning and Management Infrastructure 31

2. Training 35
   2.1 Training Supply 35
   2.2 Project Development and Implementation 43
   2.3 Choosing Training Delivery Systems 50
   2.4 Different Training Pedagogical Approaches 57
   2.5 Changing Sectoral Priorities 61

3. Manpower Planning and Job Creation 65
   3.1 National Level Manpower Training: What It Is and What It Will Be in the 1990s 65
   3.2 Creating Work and Jobs: Different Needs, Clients and Programmes 71

4. Technology for Education and Training: An Overview 75
   4.1 An Agenda of Priorities for the Coming Decade 75
   4.2 Using Technology to Meet the Challenges in Education and Training 81
   4.3 Requirements for Success 89

5. An Assessment of Specific Technologies for Education and Training 97
   5.1 Print 98
   5.2 Radio 103
   5.3 Radiovision and Tape-Slide 109
   5.4 Television 112
   5.5 Teleconferencing 117
   5.6 Computers 124

	5.7	Interactive Videodisc	139
	5.8	Hand-held Electronic Devices	143
	5.9	Film and Filmstrips	146
6.	The Role of the United Nations Development Programme		149
	6.1	Establish Clear Guidelines for UNDP-funded Education and Training Sector Projects	150
	6.2	Organize an International Education and Training Programme Consultative Council	151
	6.3	Provide Support for Areas of Need Not Being Addressed by Other Donors	153
	6.4	Promote Responses to the Challenge of Financial Stringency	155

List of References 163

Annex I: Policy Survey 179

    Methodology 179
    Trends in Education and Training: Salient Policy
        Statements from the Survey Results 181
    Basic Data Analysis: Education Survey 182
    Basic Data Analysis: Training 188
    Basic Data Analysis: Technology 193
    Basic Data Analysis: Technology Assistance 195
    Policy Survey Data 197

Annex II: Trends in Government Expenditures and Foreign Aid for Education and Training

    Share of Central Government Expenditure 231
    Share of Foreign Aid 231

Acknowledgements

EDC wishes to acknowledge the distinguished professionals who contributed to the UNDP Study. Principal authors include Don Adams, University of Pittsburgh (Chapter One), Dennis Herschbach, University of Maryland and Merle Strong, Wisconsin University (Chapter Two), Russell Davis, Harvard University (Chapter Three), Janice Brodman, EDC (Chapters Four and Five). Survey analysis was carried out by Christina Rawley. Research assistance and advice were provided by Ibrahim Ahmad, Nasir Jalil, Habib L. Khan, Terrance B. Neylon, and Joseph de Stefano. Two members of EDC's International Program Staff directed the study—Karl Clauset and Anthony Dawson.

Introduction

This paper provides an assessment of education and training needs in developing countries over the next decade and of the role that international technical assistance and support can play in addressing major problems. "Education" was defined to include basic and higher order cognitive and functional skills while "training" refers to work-specific teaching and learning. Inevitably there is some overlap in the two categories, reflected in the text of the following chapters.

A two-tiered approach was followed in the study. First, a group of technical experts was convened to analyze the existing environment and forecast future needs. These experts in turn solicited inputs from colleagues at relevant donor agencies such as the World Bank, ILO and UNESCO. The viewpoint that emerged from their deliberations is expressed in the present text. Second, a policy survey of 109 researchers, policy-makers, and planners from 33 developing countries was conducted. The results of the survey, presented fully in Annex I, generally supported the views of the study's technical experts.

The major themes which emerge from the study are those of quality, access and cost. The 1990s will be a time of limited resources, when many countries which have made great strides in expanding enrollments will be attempting to resolve the problem of improving educational quality while simultaneously holding the line on expenditures. For other countries, particularly in Africa and Asia, access will still be a major issue, most notably access for women.

Chapter one, "Education," addresses developing country needs in primary, secondary, non-formal, and higher education. Suggestions are made for activities which countries and donor agencies can undertake to respond to priority problems. Six policy goals are postulated: increasing the use of educational technologies and new instructional systems; developing systems for the financing of education that take into account programmatic and economic reality; undertaking initiatives to improve, first, educational efficiency and, second, equity; improving policy, planning, and management infrastructure, and; carrying out needed research and development efforts.

Chapter two, "Training," looks at a wide range of strategic

and pedagogical approaches to training in terms of their relevance to developing country needs. The point is made that when training programmes are conceived primarily as "dead end" or for the "academically unqualified," it is extremely difficult to achieve quality training. Vocational training should be put on an equal footing with general education by removing artificial barriers and developing parallel tracks which provide educational and occupational opportunity. The success of a particular training mode will largely depend on the country context in which it is placed. In low-income countries, programmes that require large amounts of funding and substantial managerial and institutional support should be avoided. Perhaps the best combination is pre-employment programmes, focusing on a core of generic skills for youth, and in-service and retraining programmes for employed workers. In middle-income countries, factors which contribute to training quality—e.g., curriculum development, instructional resource development, teacher training and instructional management—can be more readily addressed.

Chapter three, "Manpower Planning," describes approaches to the discipline of manpower planning that can guide the efforts of those who design and evaluate education and training activities such as those described in the preceding chapters. Future manpower needs will derive from social goals and population-driven service ratios in sectors such as health, education, etc. Manpower planning for industry will be characterized by two major considerations: (1) it will be recognized that the small scale and large variety of industries in developing countries make the staffing and occupational structure from more highly organized economies inapplicable as models; and (2) that the so-called "invisible" or "underground" economy generates more than half of all employment, at least in urban areas, and manpower assessments will depend as much on street level, local market surveys as on output forecasts based on formal sectoral/occupational/educational structures.

Chapters four and five respond to UNDP's interest in the role that education technology can play in addressing education and training needs. Chapter four recommends an agenda of priorities for the coming decade: the development of national education technology strategies; the development of approaches to integrate education technology into existing training programmes; strengthening the capacity of developing countries to create their own high-quality courseware; developing prototypes of successful education technology programmes; conducting pilot projects in new and promising technologies; expanding the use of proven education technology to improve education and training quality and delivery; developing information clearinghouses about education technologies' capabilities and impact; developing sources of high quality technical assistance, and; conducting research on key education technology issues. Chapter five assesses the potential impact of various education technologies.

Chapter six makes three suggestions for the role that UNDP can play to help implement the study's recommendations. First, as a major UN funding agency, UNDP should consider developing guidelines for project proposals in education and training. Chapters one to five provide parameters for developing such guidelines, which can be universal, sectoral, or location specific. Second, UNDP, as a co-ordinating agency within the UN system, should consider convening an education and training consultative group composed of major donor agencies working in these fields. Such a group could help co-ordinate donor activity, serve as a vehicle for information exchange, and as a sounding board for new strategies and technical approaches. Third, UNDP should promote responses to the challenge of financial stringency. For example, how best can UNDP help the developing countries and their donors to define the claims of the education and training sector for scarce resources against the claims of the other sectors? What can UNDP do to enlighten the millions who will be left entirely out of the mainstream of education or training for lack of means to reach them?

Finally, annex I looks at the results of the "Education and Training Policy Survey." As indicated above, survey results were generally supportive of the recommendations put forward in the text. However, respondents emphasized certain additional areas for policy-maker attention. For example, they felt that teacher training deserves priority attention; that radio and microcomputers rank equal and highest among hard technologies based on their impact upon teaching and learning; that there is a need for research and pilot activities to address school health issues; and that short-term, in-country training and technical problem-solving and analysis are the formats in which technical assistance is most useful.

CHAPTER ONE

Education

The purpose of this chapter, which focuses on the formal educational system, is twofold: (1) to describe the central issues that are and will be confronting educators and policy-makers in developing countries in the coming decade, and; (2) to suggest promising approaches to these issues and problems. Based on this analysis, it will be possible to draw conclusions about the requirements for technical co-operation in general and for the role of the UNDP in particular.

However, it may first be useful to examine some of the changes that have taken place over the past two or three decades in the conditions, expectations and problems of education in Third World countries. Recognizing that generalization across such a broad spectrum of countries is dangerous, certain contrasts between the 1980s and the 1960s can nevertheless be identified.

First, in most less developed countries (LDCs) the output of rapidly expanding educational systems in the 1950s and 1960s outstripped the increase in manpower demand resulting from economic growth. Educated unemployed, particularly among secondary- and tertiary-level graduates, have been common in Third World countries in the 1980s, a condition that frequently co-exists with shortages in certain specialized fields. According to a 1985 survey in the Ivory Coast, 37.5 per cent of university graduates in Abidjan, and more than half of the people with higher education diplomas in the rest of the country, were economically inactive or unemployed. Furthermore, for people with vocational and technical diplomas, unemployment was very high, e.g., 33 per cent in Abidjan (World Bank, 1988). The unemployment rate among graduates of secondary school or above was more than three times the rate for primary school finishers in India in 1978, Malaysia in 1979 and Indonesia in 1978 (Tilak, 1987). Brain drain continues to take place in the form of a flow of high-level manpower, and at times mid-level technical manpower, to the industrialized countries and oil-rich nations.

Second, the macro, centralized, top-down, comprehensive approach to development planning and administration has lost some of its popularity over the last three decades. Rationalistic views of planning and linear models of change have come under increasing criticism. While formal exercises in national economic and educational planning are still undertaken in central government ministries, wide disappointment with the experience of long-range educational planning is readily found among both scholars and practitioners of development. As a result, there is increased support among international donors, and to some extent among governments of LDCs, for decentralized, often small-scale, low-cost approaches to planned change. The implications for educational policies have been, *inter alia,* decentralization of decision-making, closer links to the community and experimentation with non-formal educational approaches.

Finally, the subtleties of the transfer of knowledge across national boundaries, the ideological and political character of reform, the limits of "trickle down" assumptions, the nagging question of "development for whom," and the mounting lists of negative fall-outs from endogenous and exogenous efforts to create significantly different institutions and processes, have combined to produce a new and more cautious perspective on education development programmes in the 1980s.

1.1 Issues for the 1990s

In spite of continued debate over theories of development, the demand for education will continue to be high in the coming decade. Individual expectations of the benefits and rewards from education are likely to remain high and will typically include higher income, social mobility and enhanced social status.

Because of the perceived importance of education among its citizens, governments of developing countries will keep education high on their agendas. It will be politically advantageous to meet educational demand to the extent that this is fiscally possible. National leaders will continue to argue for support of national education policies based on education's perceived contribution to a variety of national goals, including: national integration, lower fertility rates, promotion of ideological commitment, achievement of equality of social and economic opportunity and realization of individual basic rights.

Table 1: Per cent of Population with no Education

Region	%
East Africa	38
West Africa	70
Middle East/North Africa	66
South Asia	58
East Asia and Pacific	17
Latin America and the Caribbean	22

(Horn and Abrigada, 1986)

Yet educational problems of crisis proportions have surfaced over the last number of years and are likely to persist through the 1990s. Six general problems facing educational systems in developing countries are highlighted below. Subsequent sections focus on specific problems in primary, secondary and higher education.

First, little or no schooling is provided to half or more of the children in many developing countries, as shown in **Table 1** above.

Second, schooling is dispersed on a highly discriminatory basis favoring urban male and wealthy sectors. For example, in sub-Saharan Africa female gross enrollment rates are 17 per cent lower at the primary level and 38 per cent lower at the secondary level than the rates for males. Similarly, in Asia the female rates are 19 per cent lower at the primary level and 30 per cent lower at the secondary level. However, Latin America and the Caribbean appear to distribute access to education more equitably. In this region, female gross enrollment rates in primary school are only three per cent lower than male rates and are in fact three per cent higher at the secondary level. Several countries, particularly in Africa, which had made great gains in recent years in expanding primary school coverage, have begun to record declines in enrollment. This trend is attributed to the impact of structural adjustment policies, a lowering of instructional quality and a need for children to enter the work force as soon as possible and contribute to family income.

For higher education, the same pattern persists across the three regions mentioned above, with female gross enrollment rates 75 per cent, 50 per cent, and 12 per cent lower than male rates in Africa, Asia and Latin America (including the Caribbean) respectively (Unesco, 1987). Disparities in access to education between urban and rural regions within a country are reflected in the illiteracy rates of the urban and rural populations. On average, the percentage of illiterates in the rural population is twice that of the urban population and can be as high as three or four times the urban illiteracy rate (UNESCO, 1987).

Third, educational systems are exceedingly inefficient. Average repetition rates at the primary level in Africa, Asia, and Latin America are 21 per cent, nine per cent and 11 per cent respectively; the highest rates on each of the continents are 50 per cent in Guinea-Bissau, 19 per cent in Brazil and 21 per cent in Iraq. At the secondary level, overall averages are about the same: 17 per cent in Africa and 10 per cent in Asia and Latin America. Extreme wastage in secondary schools is evident in Guinea (43 per cent) and Togo (34 per cent) in Africa, Colombia (20 per cent) in Latin America, and Iraq (27 per cent) and Turkey (26 per cent) in Asia (UNESCO, 1987). In developing countries only 60 per cent of all children who enter the first grade persist to completion of primary school. This is in comparison to a 93 per cent completion rate in industrialized countries (Fuller, 1986).

Fourth, there is very little chance that universal education will be achieved by the year 2000 in the poorest countries of Africa and Asia. In sub-Saharan Africa, a school-age population growing at 3.3 per cent per year means that recurrent expenditures for primary education will have to increase from $2.6 billion in 1983 for 51.3 million children to $4.5 billion for 90.7 million children just to maintain 1983 enrollment rates. Thus, a $1.9 billion increase in recurrent costs is projected even with the assumption that per pupil expenditures are unchanged and ignoring the capital outlays required to finance new construction and maintain existing facilities. One hundred per cent enrollment would mean serving 30-40 million additional children (U.S.A.I.D., 1988).

Fifth, qualitative weaknesses are widely reflected in low

student achievement in many LDCs as compared with students from industrialized countries. Using science and mathematics achievement test scores, Heyneman and Loxley (1983) show that primary school children in five low-income countries (India, Bolivia, Colombia, Thailand, and Paraguay) scored .9 of a standard deviation below their counterparts in 14 industrialized countries. They also report that primary school children in six middle-income countries (Brazil, Peru, Mexico, Chile, Iran, and Argentina) performed .8 of a standard deviation below the industrialized country group. Such problems are usually attributed to the poor quality of teachers and other personnel, inadequate textbooks and other instructional materials, language inadequacies and various extra-scholastic factors. Without additional resources, educational quality will continue to decline in some LDCs.

Sixth, fiscal capabilities are being stretched to the limits in many LDCs simply to maintain the educational status quo. In Africa, Asia and Latin America, the percentage of GNP devoted to all levels of education is 4.7, 4.6, and 4.0 respectively. Education sector investment in Africa declined by two per cent between 1980 and 1985, while almost all the education systems in sub-Saharan Africa were expanding. A comparison of educational spending in industrialized and developing countries shows, first, that the proportion of GNP invested in education is 50 per cent greater in the industrialized countries and, second, that these spend 19 times what developing countries spend per inhabitant on education (UNESCO, 1987).

Primary/Basic Education

Primary/basic education in LDCs in general shows a slower enrollment growth rate than higher levels of education. Yet in absolute terms, expanding enrollments have created a crisis situation in many of the poorest of the LDCs. The 1990s will begin with more than 25 per cent of the relevant age cohort not enrolled in primary school. In Africa and Asia, in 1985 only 64.3 per cent and 73.3 per cent of the relevant age group was enrolled in primary school (UNESCO, 1987). Moreover, in times of crisis, primary/basic education may suffer most in the competition for scarce resources, for this sector has comparatively less political power than secondary and higher education. Limited resources in turn tend to constrain opportunities for successful innovation.

The widely-held goal of universal primary education in the absence of heavier financial outlays remains out of reach in this century for the lower-income LDCs. The World Bank estimates that sub-Saharan African countries could spend nearly 11 per cent of GNP by 2000 and still be far from attaining universal education.

Shortages and low quality of instructional materials will continue, as will the trend towards large class sizes and often worsening teacher/pupil ratios. Indeed, a recent report indicates that mean spending on instructional materials fell from nine to four per cent of total educational spending among the poorest Third World countries between 1975 and 1984. More particularly, the median country now spends only 1.7 per cent of its education budget on books and writing materials. Expenditures range from $0.80 per pupil in Bolivia to over $300 per pupil in Sweden. Problems with instructional materials in developing countries are exacerbated by limited development, production, and distribution resources; even when materials are available, they are often of low quality and may not reach the schools in a timely fashion. In Africa, 59 per cent of the countries have average pupil/teacher ratios in primary schools of between 30:1 and 50:1; 22 per cent have ratios over 50:1. In Asia, 11 out of 29 countries have average primary education pupil/teacher ratios between 30:1 and 40:1, and five countries have ratios higher than 40:1. Thirteen of 45 countries in Latin America and the Caribbean have ratios between 30:1 and 50:1 (UNESCO, 1987).

In addition, in many of the lowest-income LDCs there will be proportionately fewer qualified teachers. The situation is already bad, as shown in **Table 2** below.

On top of all this, the content of curricula will be an issue, with continuing efforts to link school subjects more closely to skills needed in "productive work." The issue of the external efficiency of schooling begins at the primary level. There has been considerable debate over the last decade on the role and structure of primary or basic education. This debate has focused on the extent to which primary schooling should pressure children to make useful contributions to their society while at the same time teaching basic literacy and necessary skills and providing more talented students with the academic foundation needed for secondary school. The question is not how to accomplish any one

Table 2: Per cent of Teachers Unqualified in Selected LDC's

Country	%	
Bangladesh	46	(prim & sec)
Chad	59	(prim)
Gambia	65	(prim)
India	37	(prim)
	20	(sec)
Liberia	71	(prim)
Nicaragua	70	(prim & sec)
Peru	22	(prim & sec)
Sierra Leone	61	(prim)
Venezuela	22	(prim)
	27	(sec)

(Dove, 1986)

of these goals but rather how to achieve all three goals simultaneously in the five to nine years normally allotted to the basic education cycle.

Exacerbating these problems will be the continuing inability to offer better salaries and more professional status to teachers, thus ensuring their continued low morale. For example, the World Bank (1988) estimates that average primary teacher salaries in sub-Saharan Africa in 1983 were equivalent to $US 2,225 p.a., with a low of $US 278 p.a. in Uganda. Average secondary teacher salaries were equivalent to $US 4,061 p.a., with the lowest salary being $US 1,003 p.a. in Mali (World Bank, 1988).

There are also growing problems in planning, management and finance. Growth in administrative and supervisory support is unlikely to keep pace with enrollment growth. Nearly all of recurrent budgets will need to be allocated to teachers' salaries. In addition, there will be an ongoing attempt by national governments in LDCs to transfer more educational costs to local communities, an attempt that will continue to be resisted by local governments. Indeed, the most pressing planning issue will be how to improve quality without escalating costs or, especially in some African countries, how to maintain quality while lowering costs.

Secondary Education
Secondary education in LDCs, often only an urban phenomenon, typically encounters a great deal of pressure from below and above. Primary education generates increasing demand for secondary school places. Higher education influences curricula and standards and often controls the preparation of teachers. In addition, secondary education is widely viewed as being in preparation for university study. However, secondary school leavers typically outstrip by a wide margin the capacities of available universities.

Assuming moderate economic growth rates, a falling percentage of secondary graduates will find employment in the modern sector in the 1990s. Indeed, unemployment of youth 15-18 years of age will probably be exceedingly high in the 1990s. This situation, however, is unlikely to curb educational demand. On the contrary, unemployment fuels demands for higher education certification. The enthusiasm to proceed to higher education will be abated only by the availability of alternative paths to acceptable careers and social status.

In secondary education, there are also likely to be problems connected with instruction and curricula. For example, the extent of major curricular innovations borrowed from the West, e.g., modern math or inquiry learning, will be subjected to considerable debate but probably will decrease in the 1990s. There will be continued, though highly controversial, efforts to broaden the curricula of secondary schools, blending general and vocational education and including direct occupational training. Finally, a limited number of instructional and curricular innovations will continue, but they will tend to be frustrated by inadequate financing and conflict over the scope of functions of secondary education.

Certain problems in the planning, management and financing of secondary education will tend to be highlighted and exacerbated. The relative scarcity of secondary education opportunities in rural areas will be of major concern, particularly to local communities and some international donors.

As with primary education, a major controversy will be how to provide education at reduced unit costs. Unit costs in 1983 (in 1983 US dollars) in sub-Saharan Africa were $48 per primary student, $223 per secondary student, and $2710 per tertiary student. Effectively, African countries are spending on one tertiary student, on the average, 56 times what they spend on a primary student (World Bank, 1988). Increased concern will be voiced about controlling the output of secondary education to reduce both the number of the educated unemployed and the pressure on tertiary institutions.

Higher Education

Higher education in LDCs has undergone a faster growth rate than lower levels of education and has absorbed a disproportionate amount of educational budgets. Higher education has been comparatively much more expensive, with unit costs running as much as 100 times those of primary education. The World Bank World Development Report for 1988 presents unit costs for different levels of education as a per cent of GNP per capita. In developing countries, costs per primary, secondary and tertiary student are 14 per cent, 41 per cent and 370 per cent of GNP per capita respectively. In industrialized countries these figures are 22 per cent, 24 per cent, and 49 per cent.

More important, perhaps, is the persistent controversy as to the purpose and functions of higher education in LDCs. There are proponents of universalization, who argue in effect that universities around the world should share common ideals and to a considerable extent common curricula. Others argue that universities in LDCs should be shaped by the development needs of the state and should therefore focus on generating and applying knowledge to priority development tasks.

Some future problems in instruction and curriculum content are as follows: great variations in quality will persist within and across countries; the social sciences and humanities will continue to enroll the bulk of students; strenuous attempts will be made to change this emphasis, raising the issue of the comparative worth of university programmes; and issues of localizing of curricula and the ill effects of transferring western content and standards will come to the forefront.

In addition, with regard to the planning, management and financing of higher education, the developmental role of universities will continue to be a major issue. Moreover, an increased variety of post-secondary public and private specialized institutes and training arrangements will be proposed to meet needs not being fulfilled by universities. At the highest levels of government in LDCs and among international donors, the policy options with respect to raising quality and lowering costs will be considered; however, agreement as to acceptable courses of action will remain elusive. In spite of debate, the primary functions of teaching, research and service will continue to dominate higher education systems.

1.2 Meeting the Challenges—Promising Approaches for the 1990's

The goals, problems and issues anticipated in the 1990s suggest that much debate over appropriate educational policy may be expected. Concern will evolve around the need simultaneously to reduce costs, improve quality and increase educational opportunities. These preoccupations in particular may result in increased attention to policy analysis and evaluation and renewed interest in, and perhaps redefinition of, educational planning. Policy directions will include the areas discussed below.

Increased Use of Educational Technologies and New Instructional Systems
The 1990s will see increasing applications of educational technologies. For example, interactive radio as an enhancement to formal education settings has had appreciable success in Nicaragua in the teaching of math, in Kenya for teaching English, in Thailand for teaching Thai and math, and in Mexico and the Dominican Republic in a variety of subjects (Anzalone 1986. For more on the role of educational technology see Chapters four and five.) Variations on the traditional organization and content of education will be attempted. For example, the introduction of programmed instructional materials and innovative organizational interventions, e.g., 20-minute cycles of direct instruction, practice, review, and one-module-a-day peer group work in Liberian primary schools have allowed individual pacing of instruction and personal sequencing of student progress (Thiagazajan, 1986).

The RIT (Reduced Instructional Time) Project in Thailand makes use of the adaptive learning environments model to improve the efficiency of instruction by reducing the amount of time demanded of teachers. The use of self-directed materials and pupil-to-pupil interaction freed teachers to give individualized instruction and permitted students to learn at their own pace. The project was successfully implemented in multi-grade schools with student teacher ratios of 70:1. By reducing teacher instruction time by 20-30 per cent at the first grade, 30-40 per cent at the second grade, and by 50-90 per cent at grades three through six, Project RIT enabled teachers to handle more grades in the same school and significantly improved the quality of instruction and student achievement (Montero-Sieburth, 1987).

New views of production-oriented education
These perspectives integrate within basic education elements of health, agriculture, housing and industry. In Jamaica, the integration of health and nutrition content into primary school reading primers demonstrated that efficiencies in learning could be achieved through fusion of content and pedagogy (Israel, 1987). In Colombia, 700,000 students in the eighth, ninth, and tenth grades spend 80 semester hours studying topics such as diarrhoeal disease, oral rehydration therapy, vaccine preventable diseases, malnutrition, complications of pregnancy and childbirth and the emotional development of children. With the knowledge gained in class, these students spend another 30 hours as "health monitors" visiting households to share what they have learned (Allan, 1988).

New levels of community control of primary education and at times of secondary and teacher education
These may lead to incremental and occasionally radical differences in organization and content of schooling. For example, in the Hebei Province of The People's Republic of China, local committees organized by villagers were given responsibility for school management and finance as part of the Rural Responsibility System which liberalized the village economy and allowed rural communities, with their increased incomes, to take over the funding and control of local schools.

The extension of non-formal education to out of school youth and adults

Distance education will provide the core medium for such instruction. A non-formal adult educational radio project in Huayacocolta, Mexico proved very successful in helping *campesinos* confront development issues and problems. This project's success is attributed to the direct interaction between the target groups and the radio broadcasts so that local *campesinos* were allowed inputs into programme content and structure (Ginsburg and Arias-Gondinez, 1984).

New Systems for Financing Education

The high cost of traditional institutional arrangements for education, together with the continuing high demand for education, have created a crisis in the financing of education in many LDCs. Any downturn in their economies would further exacerbate this crisis. There are various possible policies and programmes for reducing education costs. *First,* enrollment expansion can be restricted, particularly in higher education by raising entrance or exit standards, and/or eliminating student stipends and other forms of student support. *Second,* resources may be spread even thinner over expanding school populations by allowing higher student/teacher ratios (secondary and higher education) and by restricting the number or length of programmes.

Third, new funding sources may be sought, particularly at the primary and higher education levels. At the primary level, increased efforts can be made to get local communities to share in educational costs and make education more self-reliant financially. In higher and vocational education, expanded attention can be given to user fees and loans and a variety of programmes of private involvement. The potential for cutting public subsidies to higher education (thus permitting a shift of resources to primary/basic education) is likely to be fully explored. Finally, private and employer-related education may be more widely encouraged in order to meet specialized knowledge needs.

1.3 Undertaking Initiatives to Improve Educational Efficiency

One of the major problems in education in the developing countries in the coming years will be how to improve its internal efficiency, i.e., how to ensure more educational output per unit of input. This may be attained through the following means:

- *Maintaining unit costs at the primary level by some combination of reducing wastage and improving organization:* Given the structure of primary school costs there will be limited opportunity for their reduction. In some LDCs additional resources will be necessary just to keep school enrollments abreast of population growth. For example, the unit costs of education in Burundi are to be reduced by increasing student-teacher ratios (double-shifting at the primary level), increasing the teaching workload of secondary and higher education teachers and reducing administrative staff at the secondary and tertiary levels. Government subsidies to secondary and higher education will be diminished by reducing the number of secondary boarding students through more efficient assignment of students to schools and by limiting the financing of post-secondary study abroad. Increasing parental contributions to educational financing through the augmentation of school fees will also recover some of the unit costs.
- *Experimenting with a combination of methods to reduce dropouts and repetition:* These may include alternative approaches to primary schooling (e.g., single sex schools, biennial intake of new pupils, Koranic schools), adjustments in school schedule to reduce opportunity costs for child's family, modification of standards for promotion, peer instructional support, etc. Qualitative improvements designed to increase the internal efficiency of the education system include in-service training for primary and secondary teachers and the increased development and distribution of textbooks and teacher guides.
- *Reducing unit costs in secondary and higher education:* This may be accomplished through some combination of reduction of average salary of teachers, increasing the student/teacher ratio, better screening of students, and seeking various economies of scale. In Burkina-Faso, where increasing a pupil-teacher ratio already at 65:1 would be questionable, reductions in unit costs in primary education have been achieved by restructuring the teaching corps. By reducing the number of years of pre-service

formal training required for certified primary teachers from two years to one and therefore reclassifying newly recruited teachers to a lower civil service grade, unit costs were brought down dramatically. These types of interventions are the cornerstones of World Bank policy in reducing unit costs and expanding access to education in sub-Saharan Africa (World Bank Staff Report).
- *Creating or improving national, standardized examinations to offer uniform high standards for curriculum and teaching:* Kenya's experience in reforming the Certificate of Primary Education (CPE) examination in the late 1970s showed that changes could be made in examination systems to increase efficiency, equity, and relevance while encouraging teachers to improve the quality of basic education (Psacharopoulos and Woodhall, 1985).

At least seven aspects of quality, external efficiency and relevance need to be addressed by developing countries. First, attempts should be made to improve the quality and availability of textbooks and other learning materials in primary and secondary schools. The introduction of textbooks for Math, Science and Filipino in grades 1 and 2 in the Philippines produced significant achievement gains in those subjects for students benefiting from the distribution of the books. Student book ratios were reduced from 10:1 to 2:1 and unit costs were only increased by one per cent. The success of the project is largely attributed to the books being of high quality and delivered reasonably on time, and their being well understood and used by teachers (Heyneman and Jamison, 1984).

Second, efforts to control academic standards and improve pedagogy and curriculum through use of high-quality standardized examinations and primary and secondary schools must be broadened. Kenyan students must pass the Certificate of Primary Education (CPE) examination in order to enter formal secondary education. It was felt in the 1970s that this test rewarded memorization rather than reasoning ability and had little relevance to students who would not continue their education. Reform of the CPE incorporated questions relevant to the lives of Kenyan students and for which the resources would tax skills related to reasoning and thinking. In addition, teachers were given instruction in how to help students improve their performance. The exam and eventually the reforms in the test were carried over to textbooks and teaching materials. Kenya was able to motivate students, teachers and administrators to adapt the changes and improve the quality of primary school education (World Bank, 1988).

Third, nutrition/health status must be considered as a factor affecting learning outcomes. Public health efforts in developing countries largely have concentrated on mothers and children, ages 1-5. However, recent evidence suggests that the prevalence of adverse health conditions and morbidity factors in primary school age students may seriously affect efforts to improve educational efficiency. Recent evidence suggests that the introduction of simple interventions, such as regular de-worming of students, iron supplementation, and appropriate school feeding programmes, has a positive impact on school enrollment, attendance, and academic performance (Israel, 1988).

Fourth, teacher training, especially at in-service level (primary and secondary schools), must be improved. One method, known as "Cascade Training," makes use of the flow of knowledge and advice from experts and specialists through several layers of personnel to teachers. Groups of specialists train college professors and school inspectors, who train large numbers of principals and selected teachers, who then train the local level teachers. This method takes advantage of the existing structure and personnel of the education system. In India this type of in-service approach has improved the quality of teaching in primary schools, and Malaysia has witnessed improved teaching methods and curriculum implementation.

Fifth, better support and supervisory services for teachers are needed. In Papua New Guinea, senior subject teachers (Master Teachers) are responsible for checking the lesson plans of all new teachers. Master teachers visit their classrooms, give model lessons, and encourage teachers to share their ideas. Similar systems are being used in Sri Lanka, Malaysia, and Singapore. In Benin, principals are undergoing one-year training programmes to train them to instruct their teachers in classroom management and to increase their supervisory role. In Zambia, Bangladesh, Botswana, Lesotho, Nigeria, Malawi, and India, courses have been developed to train teacher trainers. The new positions filled by these trained personnel are intended as resources and supports for teachers (Dove, 1986).

The Zimbabwe Integrated National Teacher Education Course (ZINTEC) is a multi-media approach to the training of teachers which makes use of distance education as an integral part of the pre-service training of teachers. In order to accelerate the training of qualified personnel to meet the growing demand for teachers, ZINTEC was introduced as a means to reduce the amount of time teachers need to spend in conventional training courses; it does so by providing continued instruction and support to teachers in remote areas after they have been posted. The programme has been so successful that by 1985 the conventional training programme had been abolished, and a new training programme which builds on the experience of ZINTEC had begun (Dove, 1986).

Sixth, teacher resource centers should be created, where teachers may obtain materials and training. Successful teacher centers have long been operating in Calcutta, providing full-time in-service training, part-time evening courses, conferences for principals, and workshops and seminars on improving teaching methods and classroom management. These centers are valuable resources for teachers in the field, and provide a forum for the exchange of ideas and evaluation of alternative methods (Dove, 1986).

Seventh, distance education programmes should be provided as a major alternative to the delivery of secondary, higher and adult education. The Ramkhamhaeng University in Thailand combines an open university with the more traditional higher education structure. Open admissions provide access to all secondary graduates and the university offers traditional lectures as well as specially written textbooks and media programmes for those who wish to learn at a distance. The inclusion of distance education programmes allows higher education to be available to students from a broader range of socio-economic backgrounds (Danskin, 1983).

Other areas include: encouraging at the primary and secondary levels strong general education as opposed to job-specific training; experimenting with diversification of secondary school curricula, particularly by adding pre-vocational skills, and; promoting higher quality and increased relevance of universities through higher entrance and success standards, and a structure of incentives biased toward priority disciplines and professions.

Undertaking Initiatives to Improve Educational Equity

Equity and efficiency may be closely related. Note, for example, the regressive effect of dropouts and repetition on distributional equity. The following areas provide opportunities for improving equity: improving the equitable distribution of pupils in terms of gender through some combination of more female teachers, parental education, more local facilities (primary schools); improving equitable distribution of pupils in terms of rural opportunity through a combination of more local facilities, free books, free meals, community participation, scheduling flexibility and distance education; improving equitable distribution of educational opportunities in terms of wealth through some combination of redistribution of some public resources from higher education to primary and secondary education, provision of scholarships awarded on the basis of need and institutionalization of varieties of distance education.

1.4 Improving the Policy, Planning and Management Infrastructure

For highly specialized skills, some LDCs during the 1990s may need to rely on individuals and institutions from other nations. Most, however, are well on the way to building their own capacity to meet education and training needs. The strengthening of institutional capacity, however, first and foremost means creating efficient policy, planning and administrative infrastructures at the central and, as appropriate, at regional and local levels. Necessary elements include the organizational structure itself, e.g., Ministry of Education (MOE) planning offices, etc., the quality of staff and information and analytic capabilities to conduct needs assessments, evaluate decision options and make management choices.

Strategies to improve infrastructure capacity include the following: improving information acquisition and processing skills, with the use of appropriate technology; building information systems to support educational decision making; strengthening analytical capacity to make analyses necessary for planning educational futures, including the ability to conduct sector assessments; creating an integrated planning structure by delineating planning, management and implementation responsibilities, from the local school to the central offices at the national level; developing the capability to conduct technical and managerial training programmes of varying lengths for infrastructure personnel at local, regional and national levels; and, building regional (inter-country) knowledge networks to share ideas and collaborate as appropriate.

The World Bank, as part of its project to improve the education sector in Niger, intends to finance the equipment, training and capital to improve the capacity of the Directorate of Educational Planning to compile, analyze and publish educational statistics. The project will finance training in educational planning, statistics and school mapping (World Bank Staff Report).

The BRIDGES project, funded by U.S.A.I.D., is undertaking the development of an interactive data base for the Egyptian MOE to serve as a decision support structure for the education system. BRIDGES is also developing the "HOST STEP" software package for educational planning. The package is designed to project future education needs and costs based on demographic data and the parameters of the education system.

Carrying Out Needed Research
There is a dearth of information in most LDCs on the environmental, familial and teaching-learning contextual factors on which educational programmes should be built. In the absence of such knowledge, instruction, curriculum and educational management have a limited scientific basis and often become a mix of ideas borrowed from abroad with such adaptations as indigenous decision makers see fit to make. There is also a lack of acceptable knowledge about the consequences of existing policies and the realistic options which exist with regard to educational change.

The particular priorities of research should evolve from needs assessments conducted in individual countries, although inter-country knowledge networking and sharing of ideas can prove highly fruitful. There are models worthy of examination, e.g., Korean Education Development Institute, R.O.K., where the goal is not merely to create a new office or institute with designated R&D responsibilities but, over time, to assist in various ways to organize professionals into active research communities.

Ideally, R&D efforts should be closely linked by policy mechanisms and to potential training and institutional development efforts. A symbiotic relationship naturally exists between R&D and the policy, planning and management infrastructure in terms of the setting of priorities, choice among decision alternatives, strategy of implementation and policy evaluation.

Sample areas of research might include, first in the area of planning and management of education:

- potential for decentralization, e.g., community interest, community capabilities, tensions with central government;
- policy-making process, with particular attention to factors contributing to formulation success, constraints of existing bureaucracy and system limitations;
- the requisites for implementation and institutionalization of new programmes—the effects of local participation, donor backstopping, costs, political commitment, etc.;
- cross-sectional implications of policy, and methods of financing among various social groups;
- costs and methods of financing various types of education and training programmes, particularly potential of local levels;
- tracer studies of graduates of different educational programmes and institutions, and;
- the efficiency and equity outcomes of alternative financing arrangements.

On the subject of the social and individual context of schooling, the following areas of research are important:

- community attitudes toward schooling;
- nutritional and health habits and information, and;
- developmental characteristics of children.

Finally, in the areas of instruction and curriculum, these subjects will merit attention:
- variations in effective demand for education among various segments of the population;
- multi-factor studies of internal efficiency of schools—possibly by drawing from instruments of IEA*;

---

* IEA = The International Association for the Evaluation of Educational Achievement. IEA undertakes multi-country evaluations in such fields as mathematics (1964, 1982) and science (1970, 1986.)

- relation of teaching style, teacher use of time and pupil achievement;
- interaction of curriculum and perceived occupational opportunities, and;
- generation of action research by teachers and administrators at the local level to account for the realities of practice.

CHAPTER TWO

Training

2.1 Training Supply

Large numbers of people still lack basic education and training opportunities. But the proportion of youth in the populations of the developing world is overwhelming educational systems. The demand for education far outstrips resources. The financial squeeze between even more restricted budgets and ever larger pupil cohorts further drains programmes of whatever quality they possess because instructional essentials cannot be provided. Policy makers are faced with the hard choice of opting for quality rather than expansion, because both cannot be provided. In some cases, the improvement of training quality will mean consolidating institutions and phasing out marginal programmes in order to generate funds. Despite increasing demand for training, there really is no choice: quality improvement has to take precedence over programme expansion. As Behrman and Birdsall (1983) caution:

> ...due to the failure to control for quality, advocacy of expansion without explicit concern for quality improvement is misguided—and the actual return from expanding quantity of schooling at current quality levels will be much less than anticipated.

In low-quality programmes, student achievement levels are often so low that the investment yields little return (Fuller, 1985). Students cannot get and hold jobs because they have little to offer employers—their skills are no different from what can be learned informally on the street or in the workplace. To justify expenditures, student achievement levels must be sufficiently high to offset programme cost, otherwise the investment is a poor one.

Low-quality programmes, in the long run, actually cost more than high-quality programmes. Due to hard use and inadequate maintenance and repair, the capital equipment deteriorates rapidly, and has to be replaced before it can be sufficiently amortized to yield reasonably low unit training costs

(Herschbach, 1985). For this reason, the cost of training may be prohibitively high, considerably exceeding costs that would be tolerated even in more affluent countries. Some of the poorest countries may have the highest training costs because of an inability to maintain tools, machinery and equipment adequately to achieve sufficiently high and long use.

Quality improvement depends in part on formulating effective policies; it also depends upon developing adequate administrative and management capabilities. But, most of all, it depends upon classroom inputs which impact strongly on student achievement. By strengthening these inputs, cost savings can be realized because the level of investment in elements unrelated to student achievement can be reduced (Fuller, 1985).

Another increasingly important issue is the change in skill requirements due largely to worldwide competition (Watanabe, 1986). Higher level skill requirements imply higher quality training.

While technological change is certainly altering production techniques at an unprecedented rate, as Dougherty (1989) suggests, the more potent force of change is the advent of an international market system which opens local production to worldwide competition. There is intense international pressure to increase productivity and improve quality while decreasing cost in those parts of the economy exposed to international competition. Workers design, use and maintain more sophisticated production technology.

The full effects of technological change and international competition on training and work are unknown. One result is greater demand for highly skilled workers competent in organizational, control, maintenance, programming and technical service skills. There is greater need for cognitive skills, and less for manual, production and trade skills (Afthan, 1985). But even in cases where "traditional skills" are used with less sophisticated production technology, there is greater emphasis on improving productivity and quality. The relevant trade-off is "...between the quality of training provision, and the numbers trained, with quality requiring greater priority than has been accorded in the past." (Dougherty, 1989, p. 22).

The "success" of a particular training alternative is conditioned by the country context in which it is placed (Herschbach, 1985). While relative cost is important for investment decisions, it may not be the only—or most useful—variable to consider when making decisions. After reviewing 76 World Bank investment projects in vocational education and training, Middleton and Demsky (1988) concluded that "...the level of economic development, and the consequent size and dynamism of industrial employment, exerts powerful influence on the success of investments in vocational education and training" (p. i). Training systems evolve differently in economies at different levels of development. In field studies conducted in Jordan, Honduras and Panama, it was found that the ability of different training programmes effectively to address skill-related requirements of employers was largely determined by favorable political, social and economic factors (Herschbach, et al., 1985; Kelly, et al., 1985; Cuervo, 1985). In a comprehensive review of national training systems in developing countries, Dougherty (1989) observes that differences between training modes are breaking down "...to the point where the range of possibilities forms a continuous spectrum rather than a restricted set of isolated alternatives" (p. 16). The particular training mode, then, is not as important as the combination of conditions under which it is implemented. These conditions determine how cost-effective training is, and whether or not employment demands can be successfully addressed—the ultimate gauge of training investment.

Looking to the decade ahead, the major challenge will be to base policy decisions on a better understanding of the training context. A programme's "success" depends largely on an interrelated set of social, economic and political conditions which foster programme stability, efficient use of resources, long-term development and effective links with employment. The economic context of programme investments appears to be one of the more important conditions (Middleton and Demsky, 1988).

Low-Income Countries

Low-income countries, in general, have not been very successful in implementing vocational training programmes of all types. A typical cycle is the following: donor assistance is secured and facilities are constructed and equipped; a core staff is trained, often through overseas fellowships; the programme is implemented, and; donor support is withdrawn, only to have the programme rapidly deteriorate. Development cannot be sustained for a number of reasons. One is that the income level is simply too low to provide the threshold level of support needed to operate and maintain training programmes over the long term. Projects are by necessity relatively small, but the unit cost of training is high because economies of scale cannot be realized. Flexibility is often lacking because sustained investment is not available even on a modest scale and adaptation cannot be made. Administrative capacity is often weak, and related institutional support may not always be available. Implementation at the school level is generally weak; because of low salaries, it is difficult to attract and retain qualified teachers, there is limited capacity for curriculum development, instructional materials are not available and certification and evaluation systems are lacking. In addition, the modern sector may be small, employment opportunities limited, and growth stagnant, constraining participation by employers and reducing support for training; graduates may have little opportunity for placement (Middleton and Demsky, 1988).

These conditions curtail the ability of poor countries to mobilize successful training programmes either in the private or public sectors. Non-formal training programmes may in fact cost more than formal ones and may experience some of the same qualitative shortcomings. Any successful training strategy in low-income countries obviously depends upon the particular conditions within each country; nevertheless, general policy considerations are outlined below (Dougherty, 1989; Middleton and Demsky, 1988; Herschbach, 1988).

Investments should be made in the least costly training alternatives that can be sustained over a considerable period of time. Programmes that require large amounts of funding and substantial managerial and institutional support should be avoided. Perhaps the best combination is pre-employment programmes focusing on a core of generic skills for youth and in-service and retraining programmes for employed workers. Resources should be concentrated; it is better to fund a few programmes that work well than to support many inadequately.

Major attention should be given to those elements of the training system required for maintaining instructional quality, including adequately trained and paid teachers, sufficient instructional resources, a certification and evaluation system and strong programme administration.

Administrative responsibility should be given to an agency that has the potential for linking closely with employers, that can be flexible and that can provide adequate management capability. Effective administration can reduce training costs, improve efficiency, and enhance flexibility and relevancy.

Collaborative arrangements with industry are needed, including the use of part-time instructors, joint curriculum planning, internships and work placements and incentives for enterprise participation. Collaborative efforts do not happen automatically but must be actively cultivated and supported. Only through collaborative arrangements will it be possible to address directly employment-related training needs and to contain training costs.

Investment must be sustained over a relatively long period of time, perhaps a decade or more. Successful training institutions take time to develop. Considerable experimentation must take place in order to find out what works best. There is, moreover, an urgent need for exemplary training programmes. In too many cases, training resources are spread too thinly, the quality of training is low and the usefulness to employers marginal.

Middle-Income Countries

Middle-income countries have a greater capacity to support a multi-layered training system, including a mix of public and private centers, short-term programmes, and various industrial training schemes. They have more resources. Training administrative and management capacity is also more developed, with greater potential for implementation. The factors which contribute to training quality—including curricular development, instructional resource development, teacher training and instructional management—can be more readily addressed. The general educational level is higher, with a more literate population attending training programmes. The link with industry is stronger, with a more robust formal economic sector providing jobs. Training is planned in response to employment demand, programmes have a greater capacity to make adjustments to shifting labor market requirements, and there is greater potential for collaboration with employers. There is also greater opportunity for jobs (Middleton and Demsky, 1988).

However, it should not be concluded that middle-income countries are without problems. All of the problems accompanying development in low-income countries are experienced by programme planners in middle-income countries. But there is a greater capacity to overcome these problems and to implement a wider range of programme options.

There are a number of policy considerations for training programme implementation in middle-income countries. First, the most successful training systems involve a combination of institutional forms, including public secondary programmes, industrial training centers, apprenticeship training, and on-the-job upgrading. No one training mode is sufficient. Dynamic economies need diverse ways to address manpower requirements.

Second, establishing linkages between training and employment is essential to successful programme planning. Local planning is particularly important; the needs of local employers are often not anticipated or well articulated if there is no way to channel information to planners and decision makers. In general, national manpower assessment systems (see chapter three) are not well established. Despite this, the challenge of the next decade will be to extend planning to the local level. It is through local planning that costs can best be contained and instructional relevancy and efficiency achieved.

Third, there is considerable potential to contain costs through collaborative efforts with employers. Employer-based training programmes should be established. In middle-income countries there is sufficient technological sophistication and production quality to result in high quality training. There are also enough medium-sized and large employers to support training schemes (ILO, 1987).

Fourth, in the short term, retraining and upgrading should take precedence over initial skills development. In most countries, the quantitative shortage of specific skills is not critical. The most pressing need of employers is to improve quality and productivity. Because of skills deficiencies in the present workforce, considerable upgrading is needed (Kelly et al., 1985, Cuervo, 1985; Herschbach, et al., 1985; Dougherty, 1989; Salome and Charmes, 1988).

Finally, in the near future, investments in the rehabilitation of training institutions should take precedence over the establishment of new programmes. Consolidation and rehabilitation of training capacity is necessary to contain costs, raise the level of training and improve quality.

The Importance of Basic Skills
The educational systems in many countries face severe difficulties, with a considerable imbalance between growing enrollments and shrinking resources. High rates of functional illiteracy are characteristic and achievement in general is low. One of the most urgent training-related issues is improvement in the quality of primary education. Young people with good elementary education perform better in training programmes and in the labor market (Colclough, 1982).

Large numbers of students enter training programmes with severe learning difficulties, poor basic skills and poor study habits. Consequently, they cannot profit from instruction, achievement is low, course offerings are severely restricted and employment prospects are problematic. The investment in training, even if modest, cannot be used well, and often cannot be justified by the return, which may be marginal at best.

Investment in basic skills development enhances development in general. There is evidence to suggest that a "reservoir" of individuals with basic literacy and numeracy skills is required for initiating and sustaining economic growth (Westphal, Yung and Pursell, 1981; Kaneko, 1984).

If resources are so restricted that a choice is necessary between providing either public primary education or vocational training, then the investment clearly should be made in primary education. In this case, the public sector should be relied upon to provide training.

Selection and Training
Trainee selection policy and the level and quality of training are directly related (Bray, 1985). When training programmes are conceived primarily as "dead end" and for the "academically unqualified," it is extremely difficult to achieve quality training. Students opt for training because no other opportunity is available. But the instructional level tends to be low and programmes are often under-enrolled. When selection policy favors a more balanced student population and it is possible to offer a range of technical programmes, more can be expected of students and a higher level of training can be maintained. There is then probably greater opportunity to address the complex skill needs of the labor market.

Some countries have formulated policies to attract a broad-ranging student group into vocational training while at the same time keeping open options for further education. In Jordan, for example, students from vocational schools can gain admission to one of the 46 community colleges, along with students from scientific or literary secondary schools, on the basis of the secondary certification examination. The community college prepares middle-level manpower and skilled technicians (Herschbach, et al., 1985). In Jamaica, the technical schools are considered prestigious institutions, preparing individuals equally to enter the labor market or university after completing instruction. Students opt to do both, with no apparent bias towards university. Such policies contribute to maintaining high enrollments and standards.

Critics of vocational education argue that to put vocational schools on a par with high schools which qualify students for university only results in considerable slippage, with large numbers of vocational students matriculating into university rather than entering directly into the labor market. This is considered a poor educational investment, since university admission can be gained through a less costly academic institution.

While it is true that vocational training is more costly than academic preparation, it cannot be assumed that it is a poor investment because the vocational student opts for additional education. Secondary-level vocational education can be excellent preparation for many professions undergirded by technical skills and knowledge, such as engineering. If vocational students cannot find use for their training within the university, this says more about misguided university policy than about the inappropriateness of a technical background preparatory to advanced professional work.

An added factor to consider is that when vocational training is seen as providing a way for individuals to ascend the path of social and economic opportunity to higher levels of training and employment, considerable pressure is taken off the general educational system (Braun, 1987). Put another way, to the extent that vocational education is perceived as limiting opportunity, there is considerably greater social demand for the build-up of general education. As Psacharopoulos (1987) rightly observes, parents may be a better judge than planners of where opportunity lies when they counsel their children to avoid what is perceived as "dead end" training. However, this does not necessarily mean that public vocational education should be eliminated in favor of expanded general education; many countries are plagued with large numbers of unemployed and underemployed products of the general educational system. What it means is that vocational training must be put on equal footing with general education by removing artificial barriers and by developing parallel tracks, both of which provide educational and occupational opportunity.

2.2 Project Development and Implementation

One of the more significant challenges over the next decade is to improve methods of project development and implementation. At least two decades of experience with technical co-operation related to the field of training has provided insights into how to structure projects in order to achieve more effective implementation. While it is true that between now and the year 2000 new ways of presenting cost-effective training will be needed, it is equally certain that better ways of implementing development programmes will be required. In fact, effective implementation may be a more important issue than which particular training mode or mix is used.

Incremental Development
The most successful training projects are initially small and are incrementally expanded as experience is gained (Dougherty, 1989; Middleton and Demsky, 1988). National training systems take time to mature. Programmes need to be started on a scale that can be effectively administered and managed until greater experience is gained and sufficient supporting staff are trained. Resource requirements must be modest until it is possible to find out what works or not, with expansion only following successful experimentation. Linkages to other social institutions take time to develop, and there must be sufficient time for training to become "socially absorbed."

The extensive Brazilian training system, for example, traces its modest beginnings to 1942, when SENAI was established to provide informal, off-the-job upgrading. Secondary and post-secondary institutions were then established, followed by the extensive expansion of SENAI (Ducci, 1980; 1983). In Jordan the training system has expanded over a fifteen-year period, starting with a combined trades training center and polytechnic and developing into an extensive secondary system, an apprenticeship training system and a 14-institution community college system (Herschbach, et al., 1985). Korea expanded its training system over an 18-year period (Middleton and Demsky, 1988).

In general, projects should be small at first: considerable experimentation needs to occur, a successful system capable of sustained operation must be established and then expansion can occur. Many technical co-operation training projects are simply too large, or are expanded too soon with too short a project cycle. It may take a decade before a country can sustain the development effort and be ready for system expansion.

Training As a System
Training takes place within a system. While the complexity and requirements of the system vary depending upon the institutional form and country context, the common requirement is that the total system must function in an integrated way in order to produce satisfactory results. When this is not achieved, the outcome is inefficiency and poor-quality training.

Technical co-operation too often has the unfortunate consequence of distorting a training system and inadvertently weakening key components. There is a failure to consider the total requirements of the system. Some components are given too much attention in relation to others, and some critical components may be ignored. The consequence is that the training system is thrown out of balance and investments are poorly used. To equip instructional laboratories, for example, without also strengthening the management, maintenance and repair capability of local institutions, may mean that an already weak capability will disintegrate under the added pressure of the new investment. Similarly, to train teachers without making provisions for adequate instructional resources means that the teachers will soon become frustrated because of their inability to make the kind of changes emphasized in their training.

Decentralization
There is growing support for the view that training systems must be decentralized in order to be cost-effective. There are two major reasons for this. First, research suggests a connection between

autonomy and effectiveness. Without sufficient autonomy, schools cannot solve their own problems, which require immediate attention and local solutions. Schools which are decentralized also have a greater tendency to develop a positive atmosphere which fosters and supports good teaching and student achievement (Corcoran and Wilson, 1986; Purkey and Smith, 1983; Brookover, et al., 1979; Squires, Huitt and Segars, 1985). It is particularly important that staff recruitment is under local control, ensuring that new staff share the goals, standards, and values of the school and faculty (Rosenholtz, 1986).

Second, schools with autonomy can more easily accommodate change. A closer link can be maintained with the local labor market and curriculum changes can be more readily adopted (Noah and Middleton, 1987; World Bank, 1986).

If decentralization is going to be successful, however, local management capability must also be strengthened (Middleton and Demsky, 1988). As will be discussed further, management training is generally an important need in developing countries, and the lack of good instructional and school management constitutes one of the major barriers to improving instructional quality and efficiency. In addition, the decentralization of authority and responsibility will involve, in many countries, restructuring what are now rather rigid bureaucratic structures—a daunting challenge. The devolution of training management has to be approached with caution, and there are no good answers yet as to how this should be done (World Bank, 1986). But failure to decentralize too often results in substantial programme inefficiency.

Sufficient Long-Term Programme Support
Costs fit into two general categories: 1) capital outlays for building and equipment, and; 2) recurrent expenditures for programme operation and maintenance. Technical co-operation projects tend to fund capital outlays, and if recurrent expenditures are funded, it is seldom after the initial stages of the project. In the long term, however, recurrent expenditures may be more important for maintaining programme quality and containing cost than capital outlays. Unless there is an adequate level of annual recurrent expenditures for teacher salaries, supplies, materials and maintenance, programme quality will deteriorate, often rapidly.

In fact, the original costly capital investment may be lost before there is an adequate return (Herschbach, 1985).

Teachers' salaries are an important element of recurrent expenditures. The consequence of low salaries is an inability to recruit and retain qualified teachers. Individuals with a combination of technical and pedagogical skills are in high demand in business and industry. Salaries must be competitive. When poorly qualified teachers are combined with a shortage of instructional resources, the result is low quality instruction. Technical programmes require annual outlays for expendable supplies and materials, such as books, graphs and charts, in addition to regular instructional materials. Student achievement is directly linked to adequate resources. Below a certain threshold of material support, instructional quality suffers (Heyneman, Farrell and Sepulveda-Stuardo, 1981; Altbach, 1983; Lockheed, Vail and Fuller, 1986; Herschbach, 1989).

Particularly destructive is a shortage of annual maintenance funds. Lubricating oil, for example, needs to be available. Broken or worn parts must be replaced and routine maintenance carried out. Unless adequate funds for maintenance are provided, full use cannot be realized from machinery and equipment. One consequence will be inefficient instruction. Students will have a decreasing amount of usable equipment available and even operable equipment will not be used to capacity. It will take considerably more time for students to reach acceptable performance levels, if indeed it remains possible. This, in turn, will lead to excessively high training costs. Because poorly maintained equipment deteriorates rapidly, it cannot be used over a period of time sufficient to amortize its cost. When the normal life expectancy of a costly piece of equipment is reduced, the unit cost of training is correspondingly increased. For example, if the operating life of a piece of equipment is ten years, but, because it is not maintained regularly, it only lasts five years, the cost of the equipment effectively doubles, resulting in excessively high training cost, often exceeding tolerable levels.

Adequate levels of recurrent expenditures, then, are essential for maintaining long-term programme quality and containing cost. Adequate annual funds, however, are often not provided through technical co-operation projects or by the host country. In the initial stage of a project, recurrent expenditures may not appear to be a problem, if project funds cover a substantial part of operating expenses, or if the host country shifts funds from other activities to cover project commitments. Eventually, however, the host country will face the responsibility for the cost of the new activity, along with the expenses of ongoing commitments. Financial obligations will probably actually increase in the long term, because new project activities seldom completely replace older activities. Upon the completion of a project, the host country must have sufficient funds to cover annual recurrent expenses or face the inevitable prospect of programme deterioration (Herschbach, 1985).

The cycle of project implementation and subsequent deterioration needs to be broken. If the project is important enough to fund initially, it is also important enough to ensure its continued success. There are at least three policy initiatives to consider. First, training investment should be based on the ability of the host country to provide sufficient recurrent support over the projected life of the investment. The required annual recurrent expenditure can be estimated from the capital investment. Ten per cent of the capital investment is a minimum, with 15 per cent a reasonable annual sum (Hanushek, 1981). The annual expenditure may be higher in programmes using considerable machinery and equipment and sophisticated educational technology, and recurrent expenditures can be expected to increase as facilities and equipment age and require more maintenance.

Second, adequate recurrent funds should be available without shifting resources temporarily from other activities to fill the immediate requirements of the new investment. Unless new sources of income are generated along with the new activity, the host country has additional commitments that cannot be met in the long term. The result is that both the old and new activity are underfunded.

Finally, funding recurrent expenditures through the technical co-operation project will ensure greater project success in the long term. It will also alter project design. Capital investment will be relatively smaller and the project funded over a considerably longer period of time. Project activities probably will also have to be more comprehensive, embracing all phases of implementation and operation.

Adequately Prepared Training Infrastructure

For many countries, there is an urgent need to repair and re-equip training facilities. Deferred maintenance, coupled with weak management, has resulted in considerable physical deterioration. Revitalization is a greater priority than programme expansion, but there is also a crucial need to prepare adequately trained staff at all levels. The lack of sufficient resources is one reason for low programme quality; the lack of sufficient numbers of trained individuals constitutes another—perhaps the more pressing of the two. In the next decade, the development of human resources will prove an essential priority. Following are a number of policy considerations.

Adequate numbers of technical teachers need to be trained. All teachers should master the following: a) use of those productivity factors which promote greater learning; b) the effective use of instructional time; c) ways to organize instruction effectively, and; d) instructional and laboratory management methods. The combined effect size of all the above on cost reduction and student achievement is substantial. With better-trained teachers, there are fewer requirements for material resources.

Pre-service training does not have to be long if it is coupled with additional in-service training and supervision. This, in fact, is probably the least costly and most effective combination. Intensive pre-service training may be as little as 10 to 12 weeks if accompanied by a planned and regular programme of in-service training following placement. In-service training is particularly important because it provides a way to address directly the instructional problems encountered in a particular training institution. Direct supervision is needed because it enables the local administrator to become familiar with the instructional problems of teachers. Both in-service training and supervision need to be carried out by local staff.

Pre-service training is a common element of teacher preparation programmes. This is less true of in-service training and local supervision. Greater attention needs to be given to both of these aspects of teacher training.

The preparation of administrators is also a priority. The lack of skilled managers is a serious constraint to improving training quality. The most cost-effective programmes are those which involve the use of local internships coupled with a rigorous selection process. The best training ground is the operating institution. Practical intern experience is particularly important in cases where candidates are drawn from the ranks of general education programmes. Administrative trainees from academic programmes are not necessarily qualified to manage vocational training programmes.

A common practice followed in many technical co-operation projects is to send potential administrative personnel into training while facilities are being constructed and equipped and instruction initiated. Typically, these individuals return when the project is well under way, or even after the donor agency has phased out its work. Management training, however, ought to occur first, followed by other project activities. In this way, the institution's administrators are involved in all phases of the project. It is in the initial phases of a project that some of the most complex management problems are bound to occur.

Another common practice is for potential administrators to undergo training abroad. This training, provided by donor agencies, includes study tours, conferences and institutional training. While these experiences are doubtless useful, their application to local programme management is limited. Those undergoing management training need the opportunity to address management concerns within the local context in which they will be working.

Some countries lack qualified administrators and the means of training them. The best policy option, in these cases, is to provide administrative support to simple training programmes. Over the long term, more complex training systems can be established and management capacity strengthened.

For all training programmes, considerable attention needs to be given to establishing and maintaining strengthened local links with employers. In highly centralized national training systems, this usually does not happen. Decisions—even those which should be inseparable from local participation—come from the top.

Co-ordinated services
When training is provided, related services enabling employers to make better use of the trained personnel are seldom also offered. Employers need to improve product quality and productivity. Training alone may not be considered among the highest

priorities of employers. The need for capital, expanded markets, better distribution networks, and advanced technology are considerations that may overshadow the immediate concern for skill training. Combined with a "package" of initiatives to address production and market-related concerns, however, training is seen as an indispensable element (van Steenwyk, 1984; Marsden, 1984). There is a growing awareness of the need to integrate training services with a series of development activities (International Labor Organisation, 1987). In the coming decade, this awareness must be widely translated into action reflected through technical co-operation.

2.3 Choosing Training Delivery Systems

At issue in most discussions about training is not whether, but how it should be done. At one level, skills need to be transferred to the young and uninitiated, destined shortly to enter the labor market. Formal schools are probably the best place to learn academic skills and some job applications of academic skills, but there is less certainty about where specific job skills should be learned. At another level, specific job skills need to be transferred within the firm to the newly hired worker. This is usually done informally, a practice which is often satisfactory in the case of uncomplicated know-how; increasingly, however, more complicated technology requires more formal and structured training. Inflows of technology make up yet another level of skill transfer; one which, in developing countries, usually comes from abroad. The knowledge does not originally reside within the firm, but must be introduced, adapted to local circumstances and assimilated. The ease and extent to which this transfer occurs depends largely on the existing capacity of the firm to adapt the new technology. Most technology has to be adapted, and new skills cannot be introduced into a vacuum (Westphal, Rhee and Pursell, 1981; Pack and Westphal, 1986).

Formal Training
"Formal training" in this context refers to publicly financed programmes administered through Ministries of Education. Diplomas are usually granted, and there may be opportunity for additional education or training. Occasionally some formal programmes are administered by other ministries. Formal

vocational training is often equated with separate secondary level vocational training centers, but there is actually considerable variation in programme types. The distinguishing characteristic is the specificity of the skills taught. In more "conventional" centers, training is highly skill-specific. However, this is not the best use of formal training.

At best, formal training programmes can respond to local labor market needs in three ways. First, the technical fields selected for training traditionally employ a large number of workers, are fairly stable in employment opportunity and form the foundation for performing a variety of jobs. These courses are offered year after year, and, while modifications are made, they are phased in gradually in response to information gained from local employers. Second, formal training provides generic training, coupled with available short-term training at the work site. That is, the training provided by the institution encompasses a representative sample of skills relating to one occupational field or related fields providing a basic technical and theoretical background, with additional skill-specific training provided on the job. Third, job-specific skill training is provided through *ad hoc,* short-term programmes, in collaboration with participating employers or groups. The equipment of participating firms can often be used. The training may be given in the institution or at the employing site, and trainees are placed with participating firms. Once the need is met, the programme is phased out.

Conventional formal programmes, however, are limited in their capability to provide skill-specific training largely because of an inability to upgrade machinery and equipment rapidly, to adjust curricula, and to focus on the varying but different skill needs of specific employers. Also, the occupational choices of trainees are usually not well defined. Formal training programmes function best when large groups are instructed in a common body of content which stays fairly stable over time. Thus there is usually a trade-off between economy of scale and specificity of instruction.

Formal programmes probably best provide training in a representative sample of skills which concern one occupational field or related fields. This was referred to above as "generic training." It provides the individual with the skills necessary to gain entry-level employment, but additional short-term, specific training is needed either just prior to, or at the time of, employment. It gives a basic technological and theoretical background, but few individuals are prepared to enter directly into productive employment without additional training, usually of short duration. The mobility of the trainee is enhanced since he is prepared to enter any number of related jobs with various firms. Instruction itself is less costly because it teaches a core of common skills to large groups, making better use of equipment and requiring a limited range of instructional resources.

The cluster concept (Maley, 1975) is one kind of generic programme. Instruction covers a representative sample of skills from a number of related occupations so that the trainee is prepared in a range of entry-level skills. Similarly, the core programme (Schill and Arnold, 1965) is based on the idea that there are skills common to a number of related technologies. These skills can be grouped, forming a basic instructional core. Subsequent skills, common to fewer technologies and forming a less general core, are also identified. The curriculum can be organized around those skills which have the greatest common application, those with the next most evident application, and, eventually, those which are most relevant to only one occupation or job.

A less common, but potentially effective, curricular option is the integrated programme: technical training is co-ordinated and integrated with supporting academic and theoretical instruction. Science, mathematics and language instruction, for example, occur concurrently with instruction in technical skills. The integrated model is particularly useful in high-technology fields where science, mathematics and communication skills form the foundation for developing job skills.

The above are a few examples of formal skill training alternatives to more "conventional" laboratory instruction. They share the following characteristics: instruction focuses on skills common to an occupational field or related fields; instruction, while more general, tends to be of greater long term value; they are less costly, since less equipment and machinery is required; they afford greater occupational flexibility to the student, since the foundation is established for entry into a number of related occupations, and; they require additional short-term training either prior to or immediately upon entering work.

The criticism that trainees are not prepared to go

immediately and directly into employment proves largely misleading. The intent is to provide broad training, and skills are not always taught to high-performance levels. Depth of instruction is traded for broad coverage, enhancing an individual's ability to assimilate additional training, a capability that is less developed by the firm-specific training that employers generally provide (Herschbach, 1984).

There is a place for specific skill development in the vocational school. To be justified, however, formal programmes must provide skills training that is not normally otherwise accessible, either because of the particular population served or the technology covered. When students can obtain informally in the marketplace the same skills taught in the school, the training investment cannot be easily defended. Training programme quality, then, must be high, both in terms of the proficiency levels reached by students, and the kind and level of skills learned. This implies that there is a progressive leveling-up, placing training on the edge of new development. But schools do not generally have access to technology unless they maintain a close link with the more innovative enterprises within the marketplace, systematically infusing into their existing instructional repertoire a growing skill and knowledge base. Otherwise formal training responds very poorly to market needs, duplicating—sometimes very badly—training that can be obtained more quickly and at less cost somewhere else.

For this reason, skill-specific training should be delivered through programmes which share facilities and equipment with industry, interchanging technology and instructors, and using a variety of co-operating arrangements. This will markedly reduce the cost of training. However, many developing countries simply do not possess a mix of industrial and business establishments with operations of sufficient quality to function as potential co-operating partners in training.

Skill-specific training should be de-emphasized in formal training programmes. Students have not made definite career choices; there is an inability to upgrade expensive machinery and equipment, thus restricting a flexible response to the specific skill requirements of employers; the training population is usually not large enough to achieve economies of scale; and the link to employment is usually not well defined.

If skill-specific training is to be provided, it can best be given in conjunction with employers. Cost is lower, since the equipment of the workplace can be used; there is greater training flexibility; the training population can be relatively small; and job placement directly follows training. Programmes are phased out when the need no longer exists.

Non-formal Training
Like formal training, non-formal training includes a considerable array of training alternatives differing in cost, length and type of training, management support required and kind of output. Non-formal programmes are operated outside of Ministries of Education, for instance, in public and private agencies. Training is usually highly specialized and leads to direct job placement. By far the greatest amount of training occurs through enterprise-based non-formal means. It is only recently, however, that donor agencies have directed attention to employer-based training.

Some critics of formal vocational training suggest that employers can give better training at lower cost (Psacharopoulos, 1987). This assertion is not supported by actual conditions. Non-formal programmes with like characteristics cost more than formal ones: economies of scale cannot be realized and staff costs are generally higher. Moreover, non-formal programmes experience the same difficulties in maintaining quality as formal programmes (Zymelman, 1976; Corvalan, 1977; Castro, 1979; Herschbach, et al., 1985; Metcalf, 1985). Of course, there are low-cost ways to train in industry, but these programmes cannot be compared directly. Employers, however, can give training to fit their needs, and are generally more flexible.

There is a variety of training activities conducted by large firms on an *ad hoc* basis, often improvised to fill an urgent and specific need. These activities may range from short-term, low-skill training under direct job supervision to more organized and structured forms of training, such as vestibule programmes. Large firms with close connections to international firms and trade associations tend to have access to training resources. The capital investment required for training is generally low because use is made of the firm's equipment and facilities. This also keeps recurrent expenditures low. On the other hand, as just discussed, unit costs in large firms with organized training departments can approach or exceed formal training school costs as the programme takes on similar characteristics: a training director, permanent training staff, special facilities and so forth. Although in-firm training programmes generally have more resources and higher-quality programmes, they cannot capitalize on economies of scale to the same extent as formal training programmes. It is reasonable to expect organized non-formal training typically to cost more per training hour than its formal counterpart. Larger firms also have few problems with retaining trained staff and thus have more incentive to train. They can pay good wages, promote from within the firm, and offer more job security and better working conditions. Some firms may address a number of skill levels through training. Their greatest need, however, may be to retrain and upgrade in order to achieve better quality and productivity.

In general, training investments do not have to be directed to large firms. Such firms have both the resources and capability to train. Large firms tend to want recruits from formal programmes to have more generic vocational training and basic education skills, with the firm taking responsibility for special skill training once the individual is employed. This is particularly true of firms with internal labor markets—the individual gains promotion through experience and training within the firm.

Small and medium-size enterprises
Clearly, small and medium-size enterprises encounter the most difficult training-related problems. Small firms tend to have few resources to plow back into training, particularly when the benefits are uncertain and long term. If employees become too proficient, they will be likely to desert the firm to seek higher-paying jobs elsewhere, or even open competitive enterprises. Their newly acquired-skills make them premium employees. Additional training must be accompanied by commensurate rewards, and a lack of promotion or new responsibilities will only hasten departure. Many small employers are reluctant to train simply because they will often face the choice of paying higher wages or losing employees. Also, the real cost of training is high because small firms cannot capitalize on economies of scale. At most, they may need to train only a few employees, and it is uneconomical to request outside assistance at the job site. Small and medium-size firms also tend to be outside the mainstream of technological

innovation and change and consequently do not have ready access to new knowledge and practice.

For these reasons, few small and medium-size firms establish organized training. They tend to rely on informal, unsystematic, on-the-job training (OJT) or apprenticeship and often compete intensely with similar firms for labor. In terms of sheer numbers, more individuals are probably trained through OJT and informal apprenticeship than through any other training means. Small firms also tend to rely heavily on formal vocational training programmes for individuals who have at least the foundation skills on which productive, on-the-job training can be built.

In general, smaller employers want specific skills taught, and rely on training institutions to supply individuals who can immediately go to work, with little in-firm training. They also rely on workers from training institutions to introduce new skills into the firm. Smaller employers may also consider the equipment and processes taught in training too sophisticated for their production techniques.

The training need of many employers, however, is for skill upgrading rather than for entry-level employment. They want a better quality work force, one that is motivated, able to respond to changing needs, capable of higher quality work and productive. For many firms, the need to upgrade the existing work force—one to which formal programmes have generally not responded—far outweighs any need for initial training of workers. Small firms simply do not often have the capability to upgrade in-house.

One of the first prerequisites of providing training for small firms is the ability to form groups large enough to provide economical training. This means that trainees have to be selected from a number of small employers with similar requirements.

Training can be responsive to the training needs of small firms if certain conditions are met. First, course material must be directly applicable to the specific and immediate training-related needs of the firm. This means that training often has to be tailor-made. While it is true that some content can be generalized across different training programmes, in many instances substantial tailoring will have to take place in order to achieve the specific configuration required by the small enterprise. Second, training has to be accessible to the small business. This means that courses may have to be offered in the evening, at the work site, in various time blocks or in other "unconventional" ways. Third, the burden rests with the formal institution to initiate contacts, to reach out aggressively and offer services to employers who may have little knowledge of what assistance they need or can get. Fourth, it is best to offer an integrated "package," in which training is part of a range of services. Training may only be effective if it is conceived and implemented within the framework of addressing other problems in the firm, such as marketing and product quality (Marsden, 1984; Herschbach, 1985; International Labor Organisation, 1987).

While generic training offered through formal programmes is sufficient for large enterprises, it is insufficient for small firms. Small firms want specific skill training. It is not possible to address the specificity of training required through large programmes with standardized content; short-term, highly specialized courses are needed. This suggests a two-stage strategy: generic training supplied through institutions, followed by specific, short-term training at the time of employment. Presently, however, the biggest barrier to such a strategy is probably bureaucratic inflexibility; considerable innovation and coordination are required. In any case, the major thrust of training activities in the next decade should be directed to small and medium-sized firms. They need services, and, in addition, there is considerable potential for improved quality, increased productivity and expanded employment opportunity.

2.4 Different Training Pedagogical Approaches

Following are a number of training pedagogies, briefly reviewed to illustrate some of the kinds of options available to policymakers.

Accelerated Training
Accelerated training, also commonly referred to as short term, is potentially an effective means of linking employers with organized training. Programmes may range from a few weeks to months, and are phased in and out according to need. The existing facilities and equipment of industry are used, and teaching staff are hired part time, often from co-operating firms. Enrollment is limited to employees or potential employees of a firm or group of firms. Employers participate in course development, which is

limited only to the specific skills needed.

The co-ordinating agency, often a formal institution, provides long-term administrative co-ordination, train potential instructors, assists in developing the programme and locates training resources. Costs are relatively modest since existing facilities and part-time staff are used.

By building on skills that trainees already have, accelerated training can produce high skill levels. One potential use is with unemployed and underemployed secondary and university graduates who have a good educational background but no specialized technical skills. High technology production, in particular, makes use of accelerated training when coupled with sufficient technological knowledge.

Structured Apprenticeship

Jordan has successfully pioneered the concept of a structured apprenticeship programme, combining formal instruction with on-site work placements (Herschbach, et al., 1985). Following an initial six to ten weeks of preparatory instruction, trainees are placed on the job. Typically, three days on the job are followed by three days of instruction, but the pattern may vary. Formal instruction is divided equally between general education, theory and practical work. A contract is drawn up with employers specifying wages and type and length of training. The apprentice is assigned to a work group and is supervised by a fellow employee.

In the case of large firms, classroom instruction is often given within the firm by an instructor of the firm. Apprentices assigned to small firms return to a center for formal instruction. A key factor in both large and small firms is the training officer. This individual supervises instruction, provides a liaison with employers, and negotiates training agreements. In large firms, the training officer works directly with the in-firm instructor, making sure that the education and training objectives are met. In small firms, the training officer works between the employer and the off-site instructor. At the same time, the training officer monitors the progress of the trainee on the job, offering technical assistance to the employer, observing student progress and providing on-the-job instruction which the employer is unable to give. The advice and assistance provided by the training officer is, for small employers, an added benefit of the programme.

Cost savings are achieved by the government because employers contribute more than one half of the training cost in trainee wages, instructor salaries and facility use. A direct response to employment needs is achieved because, once installed in a job, the trainee quickly becomes productive, and the time between the need and the delivery of such workers is markedly shortened. Finally, supply and demand are functionally related, since employers take on as many trainees as they need and are willing to pay for.

Production Activities
Production activities are a viable alternative for low-income countries. Training is fully integrated with the production of saleable products. Indigenous or "waste" materials are used along with appropriate technology. The design, development, production, marketing, sales and accounting functions are carried out by trainees, so they can gain experience which will help them in establishing their own small businesses. At the same time, the trainees generate income, thus offsetting training cost. Van Steenwyk (1985) reports, for example, that in Honduras private voluntary organizations produced up to US $800 in goods and services per student, thus financing a considerable part of the training costs.

The Botswana Brigades are a rural-based training scheme. The small, autonomous training and production units are controlled by a local board of trustees. Training is given to 16-18 year old primary school leavers and focuses mainly on local occupations. One day is spent on academic upgrading and trade theory and four days are assigned to practical work. The service and production activities of the units provide a way to offset training costs and often include community development activities. The objective is to generate income, support community development and provide practical training (USAID, 1984).

Production activities contain a natural link between the training and the buyers of the product (surrogate employers). As products are designed, produced and marketed, the necessary technical skills for each step are identified and can be built into the instruction. This mechanism allows instruction to be adjusted on an ongoing basis. Moreover, instruction is directly tied to its application. In fact, because they have more control over the design of instruction and wider arrays of practical activities to offer trainees, production centers can achieve a more satisfactory combination of theoretical and practical instruction than conventional on-the-job training.

The Service Center
The service center is a variation of the extension model popularized by agricultural services; it represents yet another way to address the needs of small firms. These centers operate from a fixed location and provide a full range of services which may include: supplying or locating training; providing credit and financial services; assisting employers with marketing and distribution, and; providing information on technical development. This alternative is relatively costly, and it cannot be expected that expenses will be recovered through user fees. Small employers simply do not have the financial resources, and they will opt not to use the services instead of paying fees. A modest but stable source of support is needed. However, when certain critical sectors of the economy are targeted, the service center may be a justified investment, since it provides a way to bring coordinated services to employers who might otherwise fail (Marsden, 1984; Corvalan, 1983; McLaughlin, 1979).

Training Centers
Training centers designed to address employment-related needs of firms can take different forms. The common purpose, however, is to provide a flexible response to the very diverse training requirements of different employers. Training activities may include correspondence courses, short-term formal training, apprenticeship programmes, conferences, seminars and in-house demonstrations, in addition to "regular" programmes (Staley, 1971; Corvalan, 1979; Squire, 1981; Ducci, 1983; Salome and Charmes, 1988). Usually a national training authority is established, with a system of individual centers under its responsibility. Members of the authority are often representatives from trade associations, unions, professional organizations and government. Operations are commonly financed through a payroll tax.

Centers can effectively centralize and disseminate information, and they can provide training resources, drawing from knowledge of advanced technology and production techniques.

Instruction can be given on-site or at the center. Strong administrative and managerial capacity, however, is required. Cost is relatively high, but this is usually shared among a number of firms. Centers may also draw from the capabilities of public programmes or individual firms.

2.5 Changing Sectoral Priorities

At an earlier and perhaps simpler time, development policy appeared certain and straightforward: rapid economic growth through industrialization would provide urban employment in a strengthening and growing formal economic sector. Rural-urban migration was to be encouraged, because it provided a way to transform small subsistence farmers into the low-cost urban workers needed to drive the machines of production. Agriculture would modernize, and income and consumption would increase in both urban and rural areas as nations embarked on the path of modernization.

Today, the development challenge is not viewed in such absolute and simple terms. Nations which were formerly food-secure cannot feed themselves; the formal economic sector has not proved strong enough to drive the engine of development; extensive, complex problems plague the rapidly expanding cities; and population growth is spiraling out of control. The need to generate greater employment opportunity is reaching the crisis point in many countries. While some nations have shown remarkable growth and development, with expanding economies challenging those of the more industrialized world, the greater part of the Third World is suffering hardship accompanied by uncertainty over the best policy course to take in the face of mounting problems (World Bank, 1987).

Linked closely with national development policy, training has primarily addressed formal sector employment. Content, institutional form, means of assessing needs, staff training, links with other institutions—all have been influenced profoundly by the perceived need to train workers for modern employment. It is now apparent that training must be conceptualized in broader terms. The dominant concern in the year 2000 will probably be the informal economic sector, followed by rural and urban development.

The Informal Economic Sector

The informal economic sector is important first because of the sheer numbers of people involved—between 20 and 70 per cent of the labor force in developing countries. Its labor-intensive activities, moreover, are a major source of employment and an alternative for those unable to find jobs in the formal economy. In a period of stagnant economic growth, the informal sector is, for many, the only place which offers any hope for earning income.

This sector is characterized by the "smallness" of the work unit, often consisting of only one or two individuals, with 10 full-time workers constituting the upper limit of informal enterprises. What is termed a "sector" is really made up of many "sub-sectors": small entrepreneurs and establishments; independent and casual workers engaged in craft work; workshop production and commercial and service jobs. These sub-sectors have different training needs, highly complicating the delivery of services because of the smallness of scale and diversity of training required.

Informal workers can profit from training and improve quality and productivity. But instruction must be fully adapted to the requirements of the very small businessman, and complement, rather than replace, indigenous work techniques. Better tools and equipment and more technologically advanced ways of working are desirable, but low-paid, labor-intensive work is a competitive advantage in low-demand markets. The informal worker competes because of the low price of his physical labor, which is less costly than machinery or equipment.

There are a number of constraints encountered in attempting to provide training services (Herschbach, 1987). First, because the units of work are so small, it is very difficult to form groups large enough to achieve economies of scale. Training must be specific to the immediate requirement of individual establishments; for this reason, general training programmes are unsuitable. Second, there are no clear policy alternatives for financing training. Presently, the trainee and his family cover the cost of training by paying "learning fees" to masters willing to take on apprentices. Organized training would involve considerable resources and disrupt a system that now provides training at lower personal and social cost than can be achieved through other means. Third, training must be accessible to informal workers. Basic educational requirements, cost, the lack of time, reluctance to become involved—these factors can hamper efforts to provide training services. Work hours are long, often spent in piece-work, and any time lost through training constitutes a real loss of income.

The workshop sector has the greatest potential for income and employment growth. Proportionately large amounts of income are generated in the workshop sectors. Increased output generates considerably more employment than other activities, and growth is more autonomous than in trade and commerce activities (Papola, 1981). Most growth, moreover, occurs not in the expansion of existing enterprises, but in the establishment of new, small enterprises. Not all small firms want to expand; they may simply want to run their firm more efficiently. Firm expansion may therefore not be a relevant training objective (Anderson, 1982).

Training policy for the informal economic sector must consider the need for a number of factors. First is non-traditional approaches. The small size of work groups, the diverse skill requirements of different subsectors and the considerable heterogeneity of economic activity suggests in turn that training must be accessible to small groups and be highly specific, while at the same time encompassing a broad range of economic activity.

Second, training must relate primarily to the adapted technology used; quality and productivity must be stressed, but this does not necessarily mean the use of more costly machinery and equipment. Finally, resources developed for formal training probably cannot be used. Resources appropriate to the production sophistication employed and educational background of informal workers must be used. Low levels of formal education can be expected. Training must address the cost, time and social constraints that can be expected.

Rural Development
Training designed to address rural development priorities faces some of the constraints encountered with informal sector training: small groups with diverse needs, requirements for specialized instructional resources, a population with little "free" time and restricted resources, and the need to address adapted technology. In addition, distance is a constraining factor. In some cases, it is

virtually impossible to form groups large enough to approach cost-effective training.

There needs to be more experimentation and trying out of instructional technology. Instructional technology has the potential to provide training to small groups of individuals in diverse locations through the use of materials that are prepared and standardized. A variety of simple hardware devices can be used with existing rural facilities. This should be a development priority.

Urban Development
The rapidly expanding cities of the developing world will present a formidable challenge well into the 21st century. There are problems of employment generation, improved quality and productivity that training will have to address. But training will also have to focus on finding solutions to a host of problems associated with managing cities. This new emphasis will shift training from being mainly a tool of economic growth to one that is applied to the complex tasks policy-makers face as they grapple with the ever growing problems of urbanization. Sanitation, housing, pollution control, health services, crime prevention, transportation—all require trained experts and workers at every level. This new challenge has only begun to be faced.

CHAPTER THREE

Manpower Planning and Job Creation

Manpower planning is carried out as a component part of national development planning in order to set targets for the education sector, i.e., the national education/training system viewed comprehensively. Since national systems of education exist and will continue to exist, some form of national level planning of education will continue for two main reasons: 1) to set targets and policies for the system as a whole; 2) to establish a framework for assessing and establishing accountability at the national level.

Manpower planning is used to provide direction for policies, and to improve the design and management of vocational, technical and professional programmes and training institutions. Since vocational programmes purport to train for specific occupations or fields, then the requirements in these occupations in the work force will be of interest. It may also help to demonstrate the relevance of vocational training to students and parents.

Manpower planning is carried out to assess the external efficiency of education and training and the relevance of training programmes to the world of work.

3.1 National Level Manpower Planning: What It Is and What It Will Be in the 1990s

National manpower planning means: to forecast economic product and productivity by sectors of the economy; to divide product by productivity (product per worker) and get the number of workers; to distribute workers by occupation within sectors; to relate occupations to required education/training; and thus to derive the education and training required in the work force. This step is loosely called estimating the manpower demand. The output of the education/training system is then forecast, and this is the so-called supply. The supply and stocks of workers are subtracted from demand to get the surplus or deficit as a plan goal for the education training system.

The basic method is only one part of manpower planning, though it is the form that has been most practiced and most criticized in past planning efforts. It provides the first approximation—the general framework—but without further analysis the structure is empty and the method limited. Planners must also analyze the unique characteristics of each sector and industry.

In public services, the product and productivity approaches of the basic method must be improved. Future manpower needs derive from social goals and population-driven service ratios, e.g., health, education, etc. In the future, manpower forecasts for public services will be integrated with general planning, and based on social goals and economic feasibility, with input norms and service ratios set by specialists in the respective fields of education, health and social welfare working along with planners. For example, food security, and the trained manpower required in agriculture to attain it, will be one such major theme in Africa. A discussion of future developments in eastern and southern Africa is offered as an example of developments for the year 2000.

Food security, based on sufficient output in the subsistence sector of agriculture and/or sufficient earnings from the export sectors to purchase food and insure access for all households to an adequate diet, will be the first goal in eastern and southern Africa in the coming decade. There the population is growing by close to three per cent per annum while food production has been declining by about one per cent per annum. Land and water resources are reaching limits in acreage and fertility. Meanwhile, drought and pest emergencies are sharpening the decline in subsistence farming, and adverse prices, balances and debt are reducing export earnings needed for necessary investments to increase productivity (FAO, 1985). Thus a more productive agriculture is needed and, to attain it, trained agricultural manpower in all required fields and levels is a basic requirement (FAO, 1984).

The requirements for agricultural manpower derive directly from the goal of food security through increased production, and from what this goal implies in technological development necessary to increase crop production, given declining productivity because of limited land and water resources. A basic requirement is for an agricultural work force trained at all levels, i.e., plant and animal scientists, extension workers, farm workers and managers.

Studies by FAO (1984) indicate substantial numbers in the agricultural work force with training (about 60,000) in countries on the eastern side of Africa (Egypt and South Africa excluded), but the majority are trained as lower technicians (certificate) or in vocational agriculture; the need is for more higher technicians, professionals and scientists to help resolve the severe problems sketched out above through research, teaching and diffusion of knowledge (Swanson and Reeves, 1984).

Based on food requirements, crop production forecasts and manpower input ratios (scientists to units of output in agriculture), manpower demand requirements can be projected. FAO studies show demand for: plant scientists (breeders, pathologists, agronomists) to develop new varieties and entomologists to devise pest control measures; animal scientists (husbandry, veterinary, breeders); natural scientists (soil, biology, land and water); agricultural technologists (Ag-engineers, agro-industry); social scientists (Ag-economists, rural sociologists); forestry specialties, and; fisheries specialists (ocean, lake, inland aquaculture).

At middle and supporting levels, requirements can be estimated and projected for teachers, technicians, extension workers and farm managers. On the supply side, sufficient output has to be graduated from area institutions and programmes, or trained abroad, to meet the rising demand to replace workers who die, leave or retire, and expatriates who are on temporary assignments. Programmes at certificate and diploma level appear sufficient, but substantial increases are required at professional and post-graduate level. Given the critical need to produce small numbers of highly-trained specialists, the scale will be insufficient to guarantee internal efficiency and cost effectiveness in the smaller countries, e.g., Botswana or Somalia. New options for supporting area institutions and programmes are required. In the past, much of the graduate-level training in agricultural special fields has been done in Europe and the U.S., but this has been high cost, not wholly relevant to local conditions and subject to fluctuation in the number of openings in overseas institutions.

The regional university idea, attractive on economic grounds but sensitive on cultural and political grounds, has been tried in the form of BLSU (the University of Botswana, Lesotho, and Swaziland), but the idea was no more viable in southern Africa than elsewhere in the world (Davis, 1980). The Southern African

Development Co-ordination Conference (SADCC), a group of nine southern African countries located north and east of South Africa, has adopted a regional assistance strategy. One country is designated as a regional base in a highly specialized field of agriculture and is assisted in building up research and instruction which can be provided to other countries which do not have sufficient demand or resources to operate programmes at an efficient scale. The chosen countries provide research and instruction and other countries receive the same. Whether this regional strategy will satisfy the drive of each nation to have its own university complete in all main fields—the problem that has disrupted the development of regional universities in other parts of the developing world—remains to be seen, but it is one alternative that must be tried when funds are short and graduates of highly specialized fields are acutely needed, but in numbers insufficient to reach efficient scale. The regional association SADCC is itself an innovative model that should be considered by other groups of LDCs.

New Developments in Manpower Planning for Industry
For industries, manpower planning will still be much in demand but in a form very different from the basic method. It will be finally recognized that the small scale and large variety of industries in developing countries make the industry staffing and occupational structures from more highly organized economies inapplicable as models. It will also be clear that a large share of the industrial product, ranging from 60 to 90 per cent, is generated in so-called informal sector enterprises (see section 2.5 above). This so-called "invisible" or "underground" economy generates more than half of the employment in urban areas, has had twice the growth of the formal sector (DeSoto, 1988) in the past decade, and, since it will continue to grow, will require major attention in technical co-operation missions.

On the manpower planning side, the approach is not to do output forecasts and assume sectoral / occupational / education structures that do not in fact exist, but to do street-level establishment and local market surveys where the methods of sociologists or anthropologists are more relevant than formal economic surveys (Davis, 1980). The need is not so much to analyze and to project employment as to create it by aiding in the development, support and expansion of the small firms that can provide the production and livelihoods in this situation.

Related to this is the need for job creation, training and guidance, accompanied by social protection, health, nutrition and basic subsistence support for marginalized groups of parents, mothers, abandoned street children and handicapped adults. The need for manpower development within a broad context of human resource development for the growing populations of the marginalized will grow, and just as in agriculture, either teams of specialists or individuals with broad concerns and skills will be required to span the need, which ranges from basic subsistence, protection and social welfare, to mass employment schemes, small industry creation with job training and support and entrepreneurial development programmes (EDP). In the years up to 2000, the optimistic scenario is that attention will shift from left to right, from subsistence programmes to EDP in higher technology enterprise. Realism suggests that a need for the entire range of programmes will continue in the developing world. Emergency and disasters will always require basic relief and feeding programmes.

Manpower planning for job creation and small industry development covers a wide range, from low-end support for subsistence and job creation, including mass mobilization and food-for-work schemes, on through training and support in mid-level technology jobs, and on to entrepreneurial development and high-end technology.

The numbers of firms and jobs in high-end technology are not large, but they exist and are critical both to develop and sustain productivity in other industry, e.g., computers, communications services and financial, legal and management services. They also represent a goal for growing numbers of graduates of higher education in LDCs. Demand for experts in job creation, small industry development, and entrepreneurial development will be brisk, but the supply of people who can actually perform in these areas is limited.

The basic objectives and entire approach to manpower planning will change from an attempt to develop a single, or even a set of alternative forecasts of specific requirements. Instead, the objective will be to develop a management information system (MIS) that will be useful for planning education and training on the basis of demand/supply/deficit structures. In addition to serving as a basis for comprehensive planning, the information system will also serve as a Decision Support Structure for management and policy decisions in vocational/technical and professional education and training.

Thus the type of experts and information exchange that will be required will be less for statistical analysts of manpower data and more for experts who can assist in developing an information system for supporting demand studies in all sectors. The information system will cover all data needed to describe the work force stock and to project demand, supply and deficits by occupation, education and training field and level. It will also include the information needed to go beyond the basic method, as described above. The important new element is not the content but the form. The data will be stored in data bases that can be updated, and arranged in spreadsheet models along with explicit forecast assumptions, in a form that will permit testing of hypotheses by changing assumptions and data and tracing the new requirements projected over time. This new possibility in manpower forecasting, and in comprehensive planning generally, yields projections that are different from the single and often spurious estimates criticized in the past. It is not simply that results are more useful, since they can be changed to reflect unforeseen events in the economy and education system; it is also that the data bases and projection models are more instructive, since they permit ready testing of hypotheses about changes, and thus trial and improvement of plans, policies and decisions.

Technical skills are required to design data bases and information systems and the models in which to use them for plans, policies and decisions. More important than the technical skills are the communications skills of the visiting specialists who must work co-operatively with the national planners in the design and prototyping of information systems that will be perceived locally as useful, and therefore used for planning and decision making. This is the new element that open and flexible planning and modeling systems permit—interactive engagement, participation, exchange and the enhanced understanding and receptivity on both sides of the partnership in technical co-operation. Thus, in the selection of visiting information specialists for the future, openness and communications skills will be more relevant than technical skills.

Work and Education: Small Industry and Job Creation

Programmes in vocational, technical and professional education and training are planned with the expectation that they will provide skills that lead to jobs; parents support and students enroll in the programmes on the expectation of acquiring skills that lead to jobs. Or students do not enroll, in part because the path to good jobs is not clear. Part of this problem can and will be remedied by making occupational education more relevant to jobs and by improving the quality and internal efficiency of the programmes. In many cases the training does not lead to employment in skilled jobs, no matter how much effort is put into improving quality, efficiency and relevance. The jobs in modern sector occupations do not exist and no amount of manpower modeling based on job structures in other economies will bring them to life in some developing countries. This will be the issue in instructional development in the years ahead. The jobs must be created, and they may never be in the modern sector or formal economy, or have the same occupational cast as in more complex economies and industries.

3.2. Creating Work and Jobs: Different Needs, Clients and Programmes

In the years ahead, technical co-operation must help create jobs and livelihood on a massive scale to meet three different client needs with three different but related programme interventions. First, work, job and small business creation must be backed up by subsistence and social support for large marginalized populations. Because of the many basic needs, the programme elements are diverse:

- basic subsistence support (food, health, security, employment), social services (family counseling) and with special components for special groups with special needs (handicapped adults, street children, illiterate adults);
- work orientation, training and job support needed for children and young adults to find work, and to stay and progress in jobs;
- support and training for creating small enterprises, finding opportunities through street level market surveys; technical and production planning; and training in management, budgeting and control of small enterprises;

- provision of credit through small loans at fair interest; counseling and assistance in locating and accessing credit sources for small enterprises, and assistance in locating raw materials, transport and storage services;
- advice in dealing with government rules and regulations and in meeting the standards and specifications of larger industry purchasing procedures;
- at the upper level, higher skill training, production analysis and entrepreneurial development, and;
- counseling and support of participants who must be made to believe in the possibility of success in the face of a lifetime of experienced failure (Myers, Brazil, 1988).

The second type of intervention is small- and medium-scale farm, industry and service enterprise development, to create and sustain employment and livelihoods for all workers, skilled and unskilled, in chronic need or in the episodic unemployment that afflicts the working class. Selby (1985) has surveyed the problems of starting small businesses in developing countries, which include: government laws, regulations, taxes and mistaken policies; the scarcity of venture capital accessible to small businessmen or to individual skilled workers wishing to be self-employed; lack of information on markets or on sources for developing market knowledge and skills; the need for help in planning, management of inventory and control; little access to needed production and technological information; little training in production processes, and; poor access to information on plant, storage and transportation infrastructure.

Programme training and support are the same as for the job programmes for marginalized groups. Working adults in skilled jobs, but subject to periodic layoffs, require less basic subsistence support but more high-skill training, retraining and job support. Market analysis is more complex, credit needs larger and the application process more demanding. Experts in small industry from developed countries may not fit the needs in developing countries where as DeSoto (1988) has shown in Lima, and Munoz and Palacios in Colombia, the main small industry and job opportunities are found in the informal sector. Quevedo (1985) and Patel (1986) make the case for one more basic element in all small industry and job creation programmes, i.e., Entrepreneurial Development Programmes (EDP).

Third, entrepreneurial development can serve as a stimulus for small and medium-scale industry and job and employment creation. Entrepreneurial development has been identified as a key element in the creation of new firms and jobs (Hirsch, 1986, Quevedo, 1985), along with venture capital to start up and expand them. Defined as "one who organizes, manages and assumes the risk of business enterprise" (Webster), the role of entrepreneur includes economic vision, business and market sense, managerial skills and product knowledge. Two other traits are emphasized: i) a drive to succeed that overcomes normal aversion to risk in order to produce a product or develop a process that is technologically and economically superior to existing ones; ii) scientific and technological knowledge that help in identifying new possibilities that are technologically feasible and economically marketable and profitable. Some part of entrepreneurship is innate, some is developed by family and cultural surroundings, but Patel (1985) and the Institute at Ahmedabad hold that the gifts of nature can be enhanced by nurture in the form of training and development programmes that do the following: i) select with care; ii) develop motivation (the need for achievement being the central element); iii) provide counseling in project development that is technologically and economically sound; iv) train and supervise to hone management skills; v) provide project and market information, and; vi) build and constantly reinforce confidence.

However difficult it is to develop entrepreneurs, to launch new and successful enterprises and to create jobs, EDP will be the central challenge in education and training in the context of international co-operation for development in the year 2000. The information that must be provided will cover a wide range of needs, clients, programme strategies, organizational and delivery forms for varied settings and the training provided must do the same.

CHAPTER FOUR

Technology for Education and Training: An Overview

All developing countries will look to education technologies to resolve major problems in the delivery of education and training in the coming decade. Yet the role of education technology will vary greatly among them, depending on the country's needs and available resources. It is beyond the scope of this paper to address the specific ways in which particular countries can best use education technologies in the coming decade. What is feasible here is to examine some of the major technology and implementation issues that every country must consider regarding adoption of education technologies in the coming decade, and to discuss the most important education technologies in greater detail. This chapter offers an agenda of priorities for the coming decade, an overview of the major technology and organization issues developing countries will face in considering adoption of education technology, and an outline of the requirements for success of any educational technology. A more detailed examination of nine major technologies, their contributions, requirements and opportunities for their use in the coming decade will follow in chapter five.

4.1 An Agenda Of Priorities For The Coming Decade

What are the critical needs of developing countries in relation to their use of education technologies? The answer lies in the capabilities and requirements of education technologies and the opportunities they pose. Here we consider needs which are experienced across countries. Investment in developing ways to meet such needs will be a highly efficient use of resources. The following key areas constitute an agenda to which developing countries may want to give high priority in the coming decade:

- developing national education technology strategies;
- strengthening the education and training policy, planning and administrative infrastructure;
- developing approaches to integrate education technology into existing instructor training programmes;

- increasing the capacity of developing countries to create high quality courseware for various education technologies;
- developing prototypes of successful education technology programmes;
- conducting pilot projects in new and promising technologies;
- expanding proven education technology use to improve education and training quality and delivery;
- developing information clearinghouses about education technology capabilities and impact;
- developing sources of high quality technical assistance;
- conducting research on key issues, and;
- developing national education technology strategies.

Creation of well-conceived and implementable national education technology strategies
This is one of the most important challenges developing countries will face in the coming decade. In order to develop such strategies, education policy makers will need systematic methodologies for developing education technology strategy. They will need training in using those methods to determine the particular "success factors" for the education and training systems of their country. To be effective, education technology strategies should reflect the input of those who will implement the strategy, e.g., school administrators and teachers. Therefore, introduction to the concepts and methods of strategy-building will also be necessary for those who will participate in the effort at regional and local levels.

Strengthening the education and training policy, planning, and administrative infrastructure
In order to develop national education technology strategies, the policy, planning, and administrative infrastructures of most developing countries must be strengthened. A fundamental part of that infrastructure is a good information system. Countries will also need to strengthen the analytic skills of those who will use the information, e.g., education planners and policy-makers.

Basic planning skills at the local and regional levels will also need improvement so that those levels can develop effective plans as part of the national education technology planning process. In many countries, it will be necessary to build mechanisms to give local and regional levels a voice in the national education policy and planning process.

Developing approaches to integrate education technology into existing instructor training programmes
In order for instructors to use education technology effectively, they need skills, values, and a sense of competency. Teachers need to know how to develop and use education technology materials so they can enrich and supplement their own teaching style, which too often consists solely of lecturing from notes. They must be able to use education technology as an integral part of instruction. In addition, teachers will use many education technologies most effectively when they can develop their own courseware (instructional materials) for the technology, even if that courseware is relatively simple.

Instructors therefore need training in basic instructional design principles for the education technology. They must be introduced to ways of using education technologies as part of better organizing students for learning, e.g., via mastery learning and competency-based instruction. Yet most instructor training programmes currently provide instructors with little or no experience in the use of "hard" education technologies. The programmes may even have a bias against education technology.

The experience of one interactive radio project is illustrative. At the beginning of the programme, teacher trainers argued that teachers would not accept changes in instruction style required to use radio in the classroom. Contrary to this expectation, however, the teachers readily adopted the radio programmes and altered their teaching styles. The teachers reported that the programmes helped them to teach better and raised student interest. Effective approaches to integrating education technology into instructor training programmes will be a vital component of using education technology to improve education.

Increasing developing country capacity to create high quality courseware for education technologies
Courseware (content and instructional design) is the major determinant of the effectiveness of education technology. Yet most of the courseware for these technologies has been produced in developed countries, and the supply of appropriate and high

quality courseware is limited in developing countries. What is sorely needed is strengthened capacity on the part of developing countries to produce high quality instructional materials for education technologies. One effective way to achieve this goal is through a collaboration of educators in developing countries and highly skilled experts in developed countries.

In addition, it will be important to encourage efforts by both the private and public sectors. The public sector alone will have great difficulty addressing existing shortages in high quality instructional materials. This is particularly true for vocational training materials. Firms in developing countries are likely to be good sources of training material that meets local needs for highly specialized technical content. They may also be quite innovative and cost-conscious. However, it may be difficult for many countries to cost-justify developing their own vocational training materials. Their potential market size is simply too small. In general, countries must have a base population of 10 million or more before there is a large enough pool of specialized potential users to justify developing technical materials. For smaller countries, the best policy may be to create regional mechanisms to develop vocational training materials for education technologies.

Developing prototypes of successful education technology programmes

Some education technology projects have been highly effective in improving quality and efficiency, in reducing costs and in expanding access to education and/or training. Prototypes of these models can be developed and disseminated among developing countries. Such prototypes would help raise the positive impact of education technology use while reducing its cost. Although the models would have to be adapted to particular countries, it is much less expensive to adapt a programme than to create one. Some of these prototypes may be complete education or training programmes, e.g., a model education radio programme to teach mathematics. Others may be prototype equipment, e.g., portable kits for radiovision. Still others may be model uses of technology that can deliver many types of content, e.g., teleconferencing systems to deliver professional training and university courses.

Conducting pilot projects in new and promising technologies
Some education technologies appear to hold great promise. Yet in the early stages of their development and use, they need to be tested in the field. Interactive videodisc is one example. Pilot projects will be necessary in order to assess the effectiveness of such technologies and to determine the programme design features that make a particular technology most effective in a developing country context.

Expanding proven education technology use to improve education and training quality and delivery
Certain applications of education technology have already demonstrated particular effectiveness in improving education and/or training quality and delivery:

- using radio along with peer tutoring and programmed learning materials to create "low-cost learning systems";
- using various education technologies as part of highly effective vocational training modes, such as the mastery learning model, learning stations, and competency-based vocational instruction;
- using radio and/or other education technologies to spread health and nutrition education in primary schools;
- using radio and teleconferencing to deliver in-service training to teachers;
- using teleconferencing to relieve shortages in advanced, specialized technical, managerial, and scientific talent—particularly in smaller and poorer countries and institutions within countries; and
- expanding distance education through education technologies.

Developing information clearinghouses about education technology capabilities and impact
One of the most important education technology needs is improved access to information about promising technologies and effective policy implementation initiatives. One method of providing such information would be an international information clearinghouse on education technology use in developing countries.

The clearinghouse would monitor technological change and its implications for developing countries, e.g., computer voice recognition systems. It would locate, revise, maintain and distribute high-quality education technology materials for education and training. It would provide information about successful models of education technology use to improve education and training and defray costs. It would provide special orientation information and seminars for national education policy-makers about key technologies, their capabilities, "success factors" in using them and examples of their use in developing countries.

Another way to improve access to information is to strengthen co-operation, collaboration and information exchange among developing countries. This may include workshops, conferences, and co-operative projects with bilateral or multilateral teams that conduct project activities in two or more countries and assess the factors contributing to alternative impacts.

In addition, national clearinghouses can be created to provide similar types of information and assistance to individual schools and to firms. Small- and medium-scale businesses in developing countries have a particular need for information on cost-effective ways to use education technology for training. This is especially true in industries experiencing rapid changes in skills. A good example of this type of organization is the Singapore Industrial Training Board, which locates, develops and distributes training materials for new industries.

Developing sources of high-quality technical assistance
In order for developing countries to improve their skills in using education technology, they need access to readily available, high-quality technical assistance, provided by individuals who are knowledgeable about conditions and needs in developing countries. These experts can provide analytic skills, training, and can act as intermediaries between developing countries and education technology manufacturers. In the latter capacity, they can provide developing countries with information on current trends and methods of assessing technology appropriateness and quality. They may also be able to negotiate for several countries in order to get volume discounts on technologies like microcomputers.

Conducting research on key issues
Finally, research is needed to identify ways of using education technology effectively to achieve particular goals. Some important research areas include:

- Assessing the true cost-effectiveness of various education technologies: all too many studies simply compare the cost of a teacher with the cost of an education technology, without considering the quality of instruction delivered. It is important to determine where education technology is far more effective than the teachers who are realistically available, and where that effectiveness offsets the technology's higher cost.
- Determining ways to serve groups that have been systematically excluded from education opportunities: such studies should involve members of those groups in the design and conduct of the studies.
- Comparing education technology use in various countries, the "success factors," pitfalls, and impacts: these studies are particularly important for education technologies that have already proved highly effective. For example, one valuable research area concerns the factors that obstruct wider use of radio to deliver education.
- Developing methods of using education technologies to provide vocational training in specific types of settings: vocational training must be linked to real training needs which are often relatively situation-specific. Research is needed to determine how education technology can be used for specific types of training in particular settings.

4.2 Using Technology to Meet the Challenges in Education and Training

An automobile bumper sticker in the U.S. says, "If you think education is expensive, try ignorance." It expresses a realization that developing countries made long ago: despite the cost, education is key to development.

During the past three decades, most developing countries have poured significant resources into expanding their education systems. The results have been dramatic. Although country achievements have differed, all have seen enrollments climb significantly. Formal education has became available to vast numbers of children whose parents had never contemplated having the opportunity to go to school. For example, by the mid-1980's, in Asia and the Pacific, primary school enrollments approached 100 per cent, secondary schools almost 40 per cent, and higher education about six per cent.

Despite these achievements, the pressure to expand and improve the education system continues to grow. The school-age population is rising and the demand for higher education increasing. There is a painful shortage of qualified teachers at all levels. Education tends to be dull and stultifying rather than stimulating.

Similarly, vocational training systems are unable to meet current and future needs. Most existing training facilities can teach only basic vocational and management skills. There is an immediate need for facilities that can provide training in the skills demanded by businesses and in the use of the equipment now being used in industry. As a result, existing training staff must update their skills and new trainers with different educational backgrounds are needed. In addition, the training needs of small and medium-scale businesses must be better met. Expanded training opportunities are also needed for those who leave the school system in the early grades, and for disadvantaged groups, such as women.

All of these problems are exacerbated by a lack of funds. As Oliviera (1988) points out, developing countries must be alert to the cost-effectiveness of investments to improve education and training; unlike the industrialized countries, they cannot afford to take costly risks. Yet they must find cost-effective innovations that will help extend and improve education and training—conventional teaching strategies alone simply cannot fulfill the need.

Education technologies are one tool—sometimes embraced as a panacea—developing countries consider in their attempts to improve education coverage and quality. Just what is "education technology"? The term is used in a variety of ways. A broad definition considers education technology to be the following:

> ...a systematic way of designing, carrying out, and evaluating the total process of learning and teaching...employing a combination of human and non-human resources to bring about more effective instruction (Ely and Plomp, 1986: 233).

A more limited, and more common, definition considers education technology as the hardware and software of instruction. In this view, education technology consists of electronic media used for instructional purposes alongside, or as a substitute for, teachers.

Here, the latter definition is used, i.e., "education technology" refers to the hardware and software of such electronic media as television, film, computers, radio, audiotape recorders, and slides. By focusing on these "hard technologies," we are observing the distinction between "hard technologies" (like radio) and "soft technologies," i.e., the "procedures and techniques" of education. It is important to note that "soft" technologies can be extremely powerful, either alone or along with hard technologies. They include programmed teaching, programmed learning for self-instruction, peer tutoring, and co-operative learning.

If education technologies are to be used effectively during the coming decade, one lesson has become clear: technology cannot be considered in isolation. It must be viewed as an integrated part of the total education system. Thus, four steps are essential to adopt and use education technologies successfully:

- analyze the needs, resources, and constraints of the particular context;
- develop a comprehensive strategy to design, implement, utilize, maintain, and institutionalize the technology. Be sure each element of the strategy fits the context: cultural attitudes and beliefs; key systems, e.g., existing instructional systems design; human resource needs, e.g, teacher training; technical requirements, e.g., equipment maintenance, and; organizational structure, e.g, extent of school decentralization;
- test and revise the strategy with pilot projects, and;
- implement a wider programme, arranging for continuing feedback and control quality.

A major mistake often made in the past has been to bypass the first step. Too often the medium is confused with the goals, and education technology is perceived as *the* solution. Instead, it is essential to start with the needs and goals of the education and training systems. Thus, the question for the coming decade is not whether developing countries should adopt one or another technology. Rather, it is how cost-effective will a particular technology be in meeting a particular critical education need, e.g., a shortage of teachers or rising costs.

After the choice has been made to adopt a technology, implementation must fit the education or training system—its culture, people, systems, and structure. Finally, each technology should be chosen as part of a comprehensive system in which various technologies mutually reinforce one another. Education radio programmes, for example, may be complemented by slides and workbooks, and infused with local relevance by the teacher.

Needs and Goals of Education and Training Systems in Developing Countries

There is, of course, an enormous variation in education and training needs among less developed countries (LDCs). Yet certain general conditions are widely experienced, and they provide a context for our discussion of education technologies.

Pressures from expanding populations, limited numbers of schools and teachers and inadequate instructional materials continue to be serious obstacles to the countries' goals of providing a good basic education to all their people. For the coming decade, a priority for many LDC governments is to develop more equitable access to education for the poor, rural populations, women and other disadvantaged groups; another is to improve the quality, relevance and internal efficiency of the education system; and a third is to develop better modes of delivering education to increasing numbers of people, including formal, non-formal, and informal education and distance education. These pressures are felt at all levels of the education system, from primary school to post-secondary school.

As for training, formal vocational education programmes have not proven to be a good investment. They tend to be expensive, unresponsive to the labor market and slow to respond to changes in demand. All too often, instructors do not know the content of the technical area about which they are supposed to be lecturing. An instructor of electronics, for example, may teach mathematics because he/she knows math but does not know electronics. Assistants then show students how to use obsolete machines. Students take tests, but in math rather than electronics.

Thus, formal vocational education programmes need to be

improved and updated. Non-formal programmes (organized educational activity outside the formal education system) and informal training opportunities (unorganized learning on the job or at home) need to be improved and expanded. All of these efforts to expand and improve education and training must be undertaken as cost effectively as possible.

What are the capabilities and requirements, including costs, of educational technologies? What are some key opportunities for using those technologies to improve and expand education and training in the coming decade? Of course the various educational technologies differ greatly (see chapter five below). Yet there are certain capabilities and requirements that apply to all of these technologies.

Before discussing these, however, two preliminary caveats are in order. First, technology alone is not a "quick fix." The most critical element determining the impact of education technologies is the quality of the content and instructional design. If content and instructional design are poor or inappropriate, the technologies *per se* will not solve the problem.

The second caveat is that different technologies work best in different circumstances. In some situations conventional instruction will be superior; in others, new educational technologies will prove more effective. Therefore, it is important to match the needs and circumstances of learners with the capabilities and requirements of the technology. As a result, an integrated multi-media learning system is usually best. There are several contributions that education technologies can offer. They can:

- expand access to education by offsetting a shortage of qualified teachers;
- provide a cost-effective means to improve the quality of education, and;
- enable learners to learn more quickly with flexible, individualized instruction.

Furthermore, as the costs for education technology drop and technical advances make equipment increasingly reliable and easy to use, the expectation is that many sophisticated technologies, like video and microcomputers, will be increasingly available to and appropriate for developing countries.

Expanding Access with Education Technologies

One of the promises of education technology has been as an alternative to conventional instruction by teachers. As such, it can provide education and training to populations that cannot be served by teachers. In general education, however, this expectation has remained unfulfilled.

At the primary level, for example, there have been few efforts to extend access to primary education by using education technology as an alternative to formal school. One of the rare attempts has been RADECO in the Dominican Republic. This programme uses radio to provide elementary education, but offers only one hour of instruction per day conducted in rudimentary schools supervised by para-professionals (Anzalone, 1988). Nonetheless, as population pressure and the demand for education rise, education technologies will look increasingly attractive as a means to expand access to education. They offer a means of reaching large numbers of people, with consistent high-quality instruction, in a form that produces learning, at a reasonable cost.

At the primary level, the most promising technology is interactive radio. The costs and quality of interactive radio makes it a readily available means to expand primary education delivery. A major challenge for the coming decade will be exploiting this technology more widely and effectively.

Other education technologies, such as teleconferencing, education television (ETV), microcomputers, and film, are unlikely to be cost-effective for extending primary education in developing countries in the coming decade. Furthermore, the content and instructional design of programmes available for these technologies will need considerable development before they will be effective alternatives to conventional primary instruction.

These technologies may be helpful, however, in expanding access to post-primary education, and, in particular, higher education and vocational and professional training. A combination of distance media, e.g., radio or teleconferencing, printed instructional materials, and occasional classes can substitute for trained teachers in areas where qualified teachers are not available.

Distance education can also provide vocational training to those who cannot be served in classrooms, e.g., displaced workers and small rural populations. Although it is not easy to provide high-quality, practical instruction through distance education, if programmes are well-designed and fit local needs they can be highly effective. Such programmes can be run by rural associations, trade associations or can be used to supplement traditional apprenticeship activities.

Education technologies can also enable businesses to deliver instruction to small groups of people in diverse locations. Self-paced, standardized, multi-media instructional materials can be cost-effective and accessible to businesses that otherwise could not train employees. A variety of delivery devices can be used, including a combination of media and teacher-directed instruction, with choices made on the basis of cost, type of presentation required, qualifications of staff and portability. Such training is usually short-term, uses existing facilities and has low staff requirements.

Improving Quality with Educational Technologies

A major contribution education technology can make in the coming decade is in helping to improve education quality. In primary schools, this is the way education technology has largely been used.

Studies show that education technology can contribute to sizeable improvements in student achievement if used over a period of time, e.g., a school year. The learning gains are due both to the quality of content/instructional design and to the delivery power of the technology (Anzalone, p. 61). Often the technology has been introduced in conjunction with other methods for improving conventional instruction, e.g., teacher training.

There has been little systematic evaluation of the impact on quality by the more sophisticated and expensive technologies such as television and videodisc. These appear, however, to vary in cost-effectiveness among different education levels. They are apparently not a cost-effective way to improve the quality of primary education, and are unlikely to be made so in the coming decade. Under circumstances discussed in Chapter five below, they may be highly cost-effective in delivering higher education.

Education technologies can also make important contributions to improving the quality of vocational training. They can provide instructional quality better than can be delivered by underqualified local teachers. They can also expand and update technical skills of both qualified and underqualified technical instructors. This is important to vocational instruction because even qualified instructors become rapidly outdated if they do not have the opportunity to obtain regular upgrading in their technical speciality. Instructors can improve their skills using education technology at less cost than through formal classroom instruction. The teachers themselves can learn from the instructional materials used with students.

Education technology is also extremely valuable for training when it is used to simulate complex industrial processes. It is far less expensive to use education technology than to purchase and have students learn on costly equipment. At the same time, technologies like microcomputers and interactive videodiscs can offer students what is effectively hands-on experience with many processes.

Individualize Teaching

Another quality of some education technologies is the ability to expand instructional flexibility. Education technologies can be designed to fit particular learning situations, and even to fit individual learning styles, thus enabling the learner to go at his/her own pace. Studies show that when learners can study material at their own pace, there are often rapid gains in achievement.

Flexibility is particularly critical for vocational training. The capacity of education technologies to be applied in a wide range of settings makes them highly "...promising as a way to address the complexities of vocational training in developing countries" (Herschbach, p. 40).

Several education technologies, e.g., microcomputers and audiotapes, offer these features. Certain "soft" technologies, such as programmed workbooks, can also provide modularized instruction, at a lower cost. Some advocates for microcomputers argue that they are far superior to other technologies—even to many teachers—in providing instruction tailored to the learning pace and style of the individual. Currently, most of these claims are greatly exaggerated. Computer education programmes will grow more sophisticated, however, and the coming decade is likely to witness many education programmes that effectively tailor instruction to the individual user. Where such tailoring is important, this technology may prove a valuable resource.

In sum, education technology does hold promise for improving the quality of and access to education and training. As will be made clear, particular technologies will be appropriate and cost-effective under different circumstances and for different levels of education and training. The questions that arise are: what are some of the general requirements for successful use of education technology? To what extent will developing countries be able to fulfill those requirements in the coming decade?

4.3 Requirements for Success

There are four major types of requirements for successful adoption of education technologies: pedagogical requirements, financial requirements, management requirements and technical requirements. Each must be carefully considered in the choice to introduce an education technology into an educational setting.

Pedagogical Requirements

There are three major pedagogical requirements for the successful use of education technologies: high-quality content and instructional design; content and technology which are relevant to existing curriculum, culture, and student and teacher skills, and; technology which is integrated into the overall instructional system.

Content quality demands careful instructional development and design. The less skilled and experienced the teachers, the more sophisticated the instructional design needs to be to deliver effective instruction. In many cases of education technology adoption, instructional materials will be acquired from outside the country. An important requirement for the coming decade is to improve the ability of policy-makers and teachers to select high quality materials.

Relevance demands that the content and the technology fit the curriculum and culture of the users. Instructional content adopted from the developed countries is often inappropriate for the developing country curriculum, culture and socio-economic conditions. This is the case even when the material is translated or "adapted." Nor is producing content domestically a guarantee that it will fit local curriculum and culture.

The technology is most likely to be relevant if it reflects the auditory orientation of learners, is creative and involves the students actively in the instruction process. The best approach in the coming decade will be to adopt instructional content that is sufficiently flexible to be adapted in partnership with local instructors.

It is often particularly difficult to develop high quality, relevant content for vocational training. To be effective, the material must provide practical instruction linked to real training needs. Materials adopted from developed countries often need considerable modification. Technical complexity must often be revised (downgrading is easier than upgrading). Tools used in the instructional material must be the same as those to be used by students. Material must often be adapted to fit the teaching and learning styles of instructors and students. Where these problems have been overcome, however, education technologies have had marked success in providing vocational training (see "Education Technology and Mass Media").

Another difficulty developing countries face is in getting access to good vocational training materials for education technologies. Small commercial markets, currency controls, budget pressures, the absence of professional organizations, and the need to adapt materials all restrict access to sources of training materials.

Thus, the ability of developing countries to create their own education and training materials, and to adapt those adopted from developed countries, needs to be improved. One way of doing so is to use education technologies to help developing country educators design content, e.g., providing templates of "short-cut" instructional design techniques and modified systems approaches (see Thiagarajan and Pasigna, 1987). Education technologies can also be used to modularize materials so they can be more easily adapted and utilized.

The final pedagogical requirement of education technologies is integration into the overall instructional system. If the technology is optional or ancillary, its use is likely to be inconsistent. Documentation, teacher manuals, training, and other support can help teachers integrate the technology into the existing instructional system.

Financial Requirements
In considering cost, it is worthwhile distinguishing between "big media," e.g, computers and ETV, and "small media," such as slides and film loops. The distinction is generally made on the basis of the complexity of development, production, and implementation, the size of the intended audience, and the possible educational significance (Anzalone 1988). The cost differential between the two types of technologies is significant.

Big media generally have high start-up and fixed costs and low variable costs in comparison with conventional instruction. Consequently, the marginal cost of adding learners is low, often lower than conventional education if large numbers of people are served. Recurrent costs for maintenance and materials are often considerable. Although costs for big media hardware are likely to drop in the coming decade, software and courseware costs are unlikely to decline significantly if at all. Providing instruction over a sufficient number of hours to justify the initial hardware investment will require a substantial investment in courseware.

Absolute cost savings from these technologies are most clearly realized when the technology can substitute for teachers. Thus, the technology can be cost-effective where large populations can learn from it independently of a teacher, or where there are scattered small groups of students and the technology makes it possible to use para-professionals rather than qualified teaching staff. Radio education programmes for adults, for example, can be cost-justified by about 2,000 students if a teacher is not required. For primary and secondary schools—where a teacher is necessary—many more students must be involved for the technology to be cost-effective.

It is often harder to cost-justify the use of big media for vocational training than for general education. The major difficulty is achieving the use levels needed for economies of scale. Instructional materials are usually specific to a particular technical skill area, and the total student population for such subjects is often small. Furthermore, instructional materials become rapidly outdated and must be replaced. The life expectancy of training courseware is usually three to five years (Herschbach).

The issue of cost-effectiveness, however, is a complex one. All too often, studies compare absolute costs of teachers and technology without concern for quality. Unfortunately, many teachers in developing countries are poorly trained and have low effectiveness as well as low absolute cost. One result is extremely limited literacy and mathematics skills among large segments of the population. Another is low value-added vocational training. Under these conditions, the higher effectiveness of education technologies may well outweigh their higher costs. This issue of the cost-effectiveness of various education technologies is a critical one requiring further study.

"Little media" cost from three to fifteen times less than big media (Schramm 1977). They fit the budgets of most developing countries better than big media, make it possible to obtain a greater range of technology and can be updated more cheaply and simply.

In education, there is also a trend toward using what are termed "low-cost learning systems," which usually include some combination of education technology (usually radio or audio cassettes), programmed teaching (good for grades 1-3), programmed learning (better for higher grades having literacy and numeracy), peer tutoring, reading assignments, self-instruction kits and some classes.

In many cases, potential cost savings from education technology are not realized because the technology is poorly used. The problems usually lie in lack of fulfillment of the other requirements of education technology, particularly those which are pedagogical and managerial. When these requirements are met poorly or not at all, achieving an acceptable impact becomes expensive—or impossible.

For example, the capacity of education technology to extend instruction beyond the numbers of students now normally served by a teacher is an important unrealized potential. The major obstacles are managerial: difficulty in implementing the required changes in teaching roles, instruction scheduling and staffing patterns (see Lipson, 1981; Herschfield, 1982; Wagner, 1982). If these types of pedagogical and managerial requirements are not addressed, the costs of education technology will probably continue to be significant add-on costs to conventional instruction in the coming decade.

Management Requirements

Management is the key to determining the impact and cost of education technology. In the coming decade, an important area of opportunity is in improving the management of education technology adoption. There are four basic areas of concern: organizational leadership; the people in the organization—their skills, attitudes, and values; the organizational structure of adoption and use, e.g, centralization vs. decentralization; and key organizational systems, e.g., incentive systems.

Strong leadership will be essential. An innovation like education technology requires someone at the top of the organization to support and "champion" its use. The leader must send clear, consistent messages in support of the technology adoption, and communicate his/her expectation that it will be a successful, ongoing part of the education system. The leader must also be able to "protect" the technology in the early stages of use by ensuring that resources are available to implement it effectively.

The people—in particular the instructors—who will use the education technology are key to its success. It is essential that they develop a sense of "ownership" of the technology, i.e., a commitment to using it effectively and a belief that it will be a valuable and ongoing part of the education or training system.

Building ownership is best done through active involvement in the early stages of adoption, including planning and implementation. Wherever possible, teachers should also be involved in instructional design and production stages or in the adaptation of the content. Teachers who participate in these early stages of technology adoption are more likely to use it effectively. In many cases, however, teachers currently lack the skills necessary to participate in these activities. Nonetheless, as a general principle, it is important to involve teachers in the technology adoption process as early and extensively as possible.

Teacher training will be critical to developing key skills and determining impact. Training will have to include such areas as: content design for the adopted education technology; effective use of the technology for instruction, and; equipment maintenance. In addition to formal training programmes, the technology itself can be used to provide in-service training for teachers, or for para-professionals who will supervise the instruction of students using the technology. Small study groups, in which teachers help one another learn to use the technology appropriately and effectively, can also be helpful.

The structure of the organization managing adoption of the educational technology is also critical. Particularly if a "big media" technology is adopted, the organization must have the authority and financial resources to implement the technology effectively. It must be able to manage three aspects of adopting the technology: instructional content and other pedagogical issues, administration and technical operations. Thus, it must monitor the quality of instruction delivered with the technology, run effective delivery systems of the technology and supporting materials and maintain equipment in good repair.

In the coming decade, an important issue regarding structure will be the need to create a balance between centralization and decentralization in education and training systems. Centralization is necessary when sizeable investments are required, achieving economies of scale is important and overall co-ordination is needed. Yet decentralization of some key aspects of technology use will also be essential, giving local leaders and instructors discretion in using the technology effectively. Developing useful models of decentralization will permit adaptation of the technology to local situations, encourage valuable modifications and innovative uses, and enable those at the center to act as a kind of clearinghouse, identifying and disseminating worthwhile modifications. Decentralization is particularly important in training activities when local employers are expected to provide informal and formal vocational training.

Finally, key systems must be in place. One of the most important of these is the incentive system. Effective incentives can be tangible or intangible. Intangible incentives, including increased attention and status associated with using the technology, can be highly motivating.

Too often, however, there are no incentives for teachers to use the technology, or to stay in the school after gaining skills in technology use. Teachers may, for example, be confronted by a supervisor who objects to the technology. In poor and rural schools, teachers who successfully use the technology are not given incentives to stay in those schools and are lured to more attractive teaching positions.

Students may also need incentives to utilize the technology.

This is particularly true for adults using distance education. Socialization activities, including monthly meetings, can help motivate students. Periodic counselling or an arrangement for graduates to receive financial bonuses from employers are some of the incentives used by successful distance learning projects for adults.

Support systems will also be necessary. Teachers must have help integrating the technology into their instructional activities, as well as ready assistance in using the equipment when a problem arises. A management information system, one that is relatively simple in its data gathering function, can be used to keep track of how extensively and effectively the technology is actually being used in the field.

Technical Requirements
Technical requirements include all of the physical requirements for operating and maintaining the equipment. A valuable first step in meeting technical requirements is to conduct an infrastructure assessment. The assessment can help identify the existing education and training delivery resources, and their capabilities and requirements for effective use. In Yemen, for example, television is widely available, and can therefore serve as a good delivery vehicle for education or training instruction.

Although technical requirements vary among technologies, a few principles apply to all education technologies. The equipment must be easy for instructors to use. There must be enough hardware and software to provide teachers and/or students ready access. Sufficient power must be available. The equipment must be rugged enough to endure the environmental conditions. Repair and maintenance must be readily available and reliable. Supplies, including spare parts, must be available.

Of course, it is essential to pay careful attention to the technical requirements of education technology projects. These aspects do, however, tend to be the easiest part of the project to implement. In the coming decade, many education technologies, including the more sophisticated technologies such as microcomputers and video, will become easier to use, more reliable, and more rugged, even as prices drop. The education technology requirements that will demand the greatest care will be those involving "human" elements. Success will depend primarily on the quality of pedagogy and management.

CHAPTER FIVE

An Assessment of Specific Technologies for Education and Training

Although general information about education technologies, capabilities and requirements can be helpful, choosing a technology requires a careful match between the characteristics of the technology and the needs and resources of those who will adopt it. There are macro-level factors, related to country characteristics, and micro-level factors, related to the target audience.

Some of the most important macro-level factors to examine are: country size (area and population); country wealth and resources; extent of industrialization; education and training system structure and capabilities; political support for education, training, and education technology; cultural values regarding education and education technology, and; information dissemination infrastructure. These factors can suggest the kinds of technology that best fit a country's economic and socio-political circumstances.

Micro-level factors include: distance of students from a school; income level; gender implications; personal handicaps; cultural implications, and; transience, e.g, are the families nomads? These factors will affect the demand for education and the response to various types of technology. The better the match between the county's macro and micro-level conditions and the technology, the more likely it is that the education technology will deliver value at an acceptable price.

The following discussion will examine nine education technologies: print; radio; radiovision and Tape/Slides; television; teleconferencing; computers; interactive videodisc; hand-held electronic devices, and; film. The special capabilities and contributions offered by each technology, the requirements for implementing and utilizing it effectively, and the special opportunities it offers in the coming decade, will all be considered.

Several of the terms used below must be defined. One is the term "effectiveness." Effectiveness refers to the impact of the technology, often measured in terms of changes in achievement. One measure of effectiveness is "effect size," which reflects the impact of the technology on average performance in some tested skill, e.g., reading or mathematics. Although the measure is not without distortion problems, it is the only quantitative measure generally accepted as a way of comparing across different groups of learners. When it is available, we use it simply to indicate the relative impact of various technologies.

Two other terms that call for definition are "internal efficiency," and "cost-effectiveness." Both terms refer to the ratio of learning (which can be measured in many ways, e.g., achievement, dropout rate, repetition rate, numbers of students reached) to the costs of the particular education technology in question. These measures must be considered judiciously because they are only available from a few studies for a few technologies, because they offer a limited assessment of "effectiveness," and because cost figures are often incomplete.

It is also important to note that "effectiveness" differs from "cost-effectiveness." A technology may be highly effective, yet not cost-effective. This would occur if the technology was very costly and alternative, cheaper technologies could deliver the same value at a lower cost.

Finally, there is "external efficiency." This term refers to the extent to which the instruction delivered by the technology actually meets the needs of the society, as reflected by such measures as job attainment and salaries. There is little discussion of external efficiency because little research is available on the extent to which various education technologies achieve external efficiency.

5.1 Print

Although print materials, including textbooks, do not fall within our definition of "hard" education technologies, we include them here because they represent a critical medium used to improve education and training in developing countries. Texts provide a standard, consistent quality of curriculum and can provide instruction in areas in which teachers are not competent. In a 1978 study, World Bank economist Stephen Heyneman argued that the availability of books appeared to be the single most consistently positive factor in predicting academic achievement.

Textbooks are certainly one of the most cost-effective education technologies—only radio has proven consistently more cost-effective across several countries (see Lockheed and Hanushek, 1988). Texts may be three to four times as cost-effective as teacher training for low-skilled teachers (Lockheed, Vail and Fuller, 1986).

One of the most attractive features of print materials is their flexibility (see Psacharopoulos and Woodhall, 1986). Print offers an extraordinary range of alternatives for presenting instruction, from technical textbooks to photo-novels and comic books. Print materials using graphics and illustrations can even be effective for those with a low level of literacy skills. In addition, print materials are easy to use and modify and relatively inexpensive. Except for textbooks, print materials are easily produced in developing countries; materials from developed countries can be easily adapted.

Like all the education technologies we will examine, the impact of print materials depends on fulfilling four key sets of requirements outlined in section 4.3 above, i.e., pedagogical requirements, financial requirements, management requirements and technical requirements.

Pedagogical Requirements
In order for print materials, including texts, to be used well, they must support curricular objectives and be appropriate to the needs and skill levels of students and teachers. Print materials are most effective when their content is organized as an integrated series for primary school (grades 1-6) and for secondary school (grades 7-12). In addition, special teachers' materials are essential in poor environments and must be practical and straightforward.

Illustrations must be used with care, because understanding the message of pictorial materials requires experience. It is essential to test pictorial materials to ensure that the intended audience indeed understands the message the pictures are meant to portray. Text is generally needed to complement and explain the illustrations.

Using print for vocational training poses certain special requirements. Material should be practical and focus on skill requirements, avoiding excessively abstract discussion. If more theoretical material is used, it should be supplemented with material presenting practical applications. All material must be reviewed to ensure technical vocabulary can be understood by the intended audience.

One good source of materials is equipment suppliers. Often they produce manufacturing materials of good quality and distribute them free. The materials can be complemented with worksheets or other supplementary print materials produced locally (Herschbach).

Like other media used for vocational training, print must be revised relatively frequently, often every three to five years, in order for the content to reflect current technical knowledge. This can pose a problem for developing countries that want to produce their own vocational training materials because print often take a relatively long time to develop. Books may take three to five years, other materials two to three years, and even simple materials one to two years (Herschbach).

Financial Requirements

Financial requirements vary with the extent to which the country develops its own print materials and the complexity of the materials it produces. Simple print materials are ordinarily relatively inexpensive; text production, on the other hand, is a complex and relatively costly undertaking. In areas of some countries, however, even simple print materials are too expensive to disseminate to all students. In the Yemen Arabic Republic, for example, many classes have student/teacher ratios of almost 100 to 1, and no print materials are available. Teachers have only slate and chalk to use for instruction. Nonetheless, print materials are generally the instructional medium most likely to be within schools' budgets. They are highly cost-effective, particularly when they can be re-used. In addition, their adoption is often supported by foreign aid.

Management Requirements

Despite major efforts supported by donors, and the annual expenditure of hundreds of millions of dollars, print materials—particularly texts—continue to be generally of poor quality and in short supply in developing countries. The major obstacles relate to management. Despite the importance of print materials, most developing countries still lack the experience to create and sustain supportable systems for providing print materials—especially texts—to schools, and the institutional capacity to produce relevant and engaging materials.

Egypt, for example, lacks an institution and trained specialists to manage its large national textbook programme and to produce a new generation of educational materials that meets the needs of Egyptian students. In Liberia, an ambitious print-based system of self-instruction failed to be successfully implemented because materials did not arrive on time in the classrooms. Moreover, the system relies on modules, individually produced and bound, which build upon each other. That approach is expensive to produce, inventory and re-supply, and is likely to create further problems in classroom management for the poorly trained teachers.

Too often, those involved in producing and distributing print materials are unaware of the complexities of creating an ongoing print materials supply system, and ill prepared to assess the options open to them. They underestimate the time involved in creating an integrated project and fail to appreciate the need for institution building and the development of human resources. Instead, concentration is often on curriculum development—often producing content at odds with the realities of the average classroom—and on providing funds for paper, printing, and binding.

Trained education managers are needed in order to supply print materials, especially texts, to schools. They require skills in analyzing, planning, and developing an infrastructure that can reliably supply quality educational materials on a continuing basis. Such managers must be able to conduct certain key management activities:

- specify learning objectives;
- plan content, organization, and format of integrated instructional materials, teachers' versions (e.g., teachers' texts) and supplementary materials;
- assemble a team of writers, along with, as appropriate, editors, designers, illustrators, and production specialists;
- pilot, test, and edit materials;
- make decisions about presentation, e.g., color, paper, binding;
- manufacture or procure paper supplies and books;
- manage materials storage and distribution;

- assure their proper use in the classroom, and;
- revise or replace materials as necessary.

In most countries, training is essential to develop educational managers who can carry out these activities.

Technical Requirements

Technical requirements vary according to the type of print materials a country wishes to produce. Printing presses may be required—an expensive and complex piece of equipment. In many cases, desktop publishing microcomputer units are sufficient to produce highly sophisticated materials, along with cameras and darkroom equipment. Although these types of equipment require trained staff, they are relatively easy to operate. Maintenance and servicing must also be available.

Small runs of materials can be produced by laser printers, which are relatively easy to operate, but do require staff trained in operations, as well as sources for maintenance and repairs. Large runs require printing facilities with more highly skilled staff able to produce large quantities of material. In some countries, domestic paper and printing industries exist which can produce the needed quality and quantities of materials in a timely and cost-effective manner. In other countries, printing may have to be done in facilities outside the country.

Opportunities in the Coming Decade

Print can certainly be a powerful tool for improving education in the coming decade. Perhaps one of the greatest opportunities lies in developing countries' creating the expertise and technical specialists to manage, develop, design, produce, manufacture and distribute high-quality texts and other print materials at affordable prices. To develop such a capacity, countries will need to adopt appropriate technologies, and arrange for those who will produce the materials to gain hands-on experience in high-quality print materials production. This will require a long-term commitment within the countries and among donors supporting the development of this capacity. This is also an area that can foster public and private sector co-operative ventures.

5.2 Radio

Few education technologies have received the accolades enjoyed by radio. The impact of interactive radio has been particularly impressive. The interactive model is designed with pauses for student responses, which have been carefully calculated by observing classes. In the Nicaragua Radio Mathematics Project, for example, the broadcast instruction often elicited 100 oral responses in a half-hour programme.

Radio's popularity as an education technology reflects its capabilities and costs. It has been shown to help improve the quality and relevance of education, to expand access to education, and to be relatively inexpensive. It has a number of features that make it valuable for distance education and more appropriate than television: much more cumulative experience already gained about radio education and what it takes to make it successful; well-established radio networks; widely-available transistor radios; a much simpler technology than television, and more easily maintained; more widely-available service, and; it is between one fifth and one tenth the cost of television.

Four types of educational radio projects have been used successfully in developing countries. One approach uses radio in school to raise the quality of conventional instruction by adding "enrichment" lessons. The second uses radio in school to deliver a complete course that otherwise could not be given. The third approach uses radio to provide most of the instruction, along with supervision by para-professionals. In the fourth approach, the learner works largely independently, using radio along with supportive instructional materials and occasional classes.

Radio has also been used for vocational training, to bring instruction to rural and remote areas bypassed by other training activities. Radio agricultural training programmes have been highly successful. In Malawi, for example, radio was used to train farmers in new agricultural techniques at costs three thousand times cheaper per hour of contact than face-to-face extension services.

In order for radio to teach technical vocational content effectively, it must usually be supplemented by worksheets or manuals. Combined with such materials, radio can be highly effective in dealing with general subjects such as marketing. It is often less appropriate for delivering specialized technical training because it requires a large audience in order to be cost-effective.

Raising Quality with In-school Radio Programmes
In developing countries, the in-school radio education approaches are most common. The audience is usually primary school students in grades 1-4. In fact, radio is the education technology most widely used in primary schools.

Experience suggests that the "total course" approach is more apt to raise quality than "enrichment" for several reasons. First, enrichment programmes are rarely used effectively. Teachers often lack the skills and knowledge they need to use enrichment programmes well. Reading materials that accompany enrichment programmes have often been of little help, being poorly designed and outdated.

Second, total-course programmes can provide valuable areas of instruction that teachers are ill-prepared to teach. In addition, in many developing country schools, there are multi-age classes. Using total-course radio programmes, the teacher can assign one age cohort to the radio programme, and teach another him/herself.

Third, total-course programmes can train teachers and "model" effective teaching methods that teachers can adopt themselves. After a teacher uses a radio course for about two years, he/she often has the skill and confidence to teach the course independently.

Impact on Achievement
Evaluations indicate that when used well, radio can substantially improve student achievement in various subjects. There are many success stories. Thailand, for example, has been conducting radio education for more than twenty years. In the early 1980's, it launched the Radio Mathematics Experiment (for grades 1-3), an adaptation of the successful Nicaragua Radio Mathematics Experiment. The programme raised student mathematics achievement significantly and reduced disparities in achievement of rural and urban students.

Guatemala used the Shuar education radio project to try to reduce dropout rates among the Shuar. The programme has been successful, making education more relevant and lowering dropout rates from 30 per cent to only a few per cent.

In the Kenya Radio Language Arts Program, children received three times as much content in a given time period as they did with conventional classes. Tests of the first grade showed that the interactive radio programme was significantly more effective in raising achievement than were textbooks. There is some preliminary evidence that rural students had greater gains in achievement than did urban students (Development Communication Report #49:11). Furthermore, boys and girls seemed to learn equally well.

The Kenya programme also showed, however, that interactive radio is much more difficult to design for grades 3 and above, when children's answers can be longer and more complex. To resolve that problem, the programme minimized the use of questions that could elicit lengthy or multiple answers during the broadcast, and had teachers ask those questions afterwards.

The Dominican Republic used its RADECO programme to reach rural students who could not attend conventional schools. Children using the RADECO programme had mathematics and reading achievement scores equivalent to conventional schools in the region, but gained in about half the time spent in learning and at about half the cost.

Radio in adult education has been similarly successful, delivering a great variety of subjects effectively, including various vocational training topics, agricultural extension and farmer education, adult literacy and basic education, health programmes, nutrition programmes and family planning. In Nepal, the Radio Education Teacher Training Project was highly successful, with participants achieving scores 25-50 per cent higher than those of regular classes.

One area in which radio has not had success is in providing opportunities for higher education to adults who would otherwise not have them. As is true in conventional universities, those who do well in radio university education programmes (outside school) are generally better educated and wealthier than those who do not complete such courses successfully.

Pedagogical Requirements
The effectiveness of education radio depends on the design and quality of the content as much or more than on the intrinsic characteristics of radio itself. The educational goals of the radio

programme must be clear, appropriate for students, and acceptable to teachers. The content must be relevant to students' experience and culture, and designed to be engaging and elicit student involvement. It must also be delivered in a language students understand. Where there is cultural and regional diversity, local broadcasting may be most effective.

Instructional design includes development of supplementary materials, such as a teacher's guide, that help teachers use the radio programme effectively in their class. Workbooks, reading materials and other materials that help students practice what they have learned also contribute to a positive impact.

Supplementary print materials appear to be essential to the effectiveness of technical vocational training programmes. All supplementary materials should be kept short so that instructors and students will actually use them.

Financial Requirements

Developing and implementing a high-quality radio programme demands that sufficient financial resources be available from the early planning stage through implementation and institutionalization of the programme.

In comparison with other education technologies, radio is highly cost-effective. In many cases, it helps reduce educational costs or at least slow their rate of increase. Per student costs of one subject—$.40-$3.00 per student per year—are close to those of textbooks. The use of texts and workbooks along with radio boosts effectiveness even higher and is still inexpensive— approximately $20-$40 per student per year (Herschbach, p. 45). These estimates exclude the capital costs of instructional development, which can run into $1-2 million over four to five years and are usually borne by donor agencies.

One of the best ways to cut costs without endangering quality is to adapt the scripts of proven radio education programmes to make them relevant to particular audiences. Another is to develop re-usable supplementary materials in place of disposable worksheets.

Management Requirements

Although education radio has been highly successful, it is important not to underestimate the complex management effort involved in that success. Programme management must produce materials that involve various skilled personnel including script writers, actors, curriculum specialists and teacher trainers. They must procure and deliver equipment and printed materials. They must be able to interact with multiple local, national, and donor agencies. Often, they must be able to defend their programme against opposition from the education establishment.

To be successful in the long term, countries must develop careful long-range plans to integrate radio education into the existing education and training systems. All of the requirements discussed regarding education technologies in general must be addressed—financial, pedagogical, management, and technical.

Teacher training is particularly important because teachers' instructional roles will change. This is particularly true when "total course" programmes are used in schools. Rather than directly instruct students, the teacher will prepare them for the programme, distribute and explain materials, help them understand the radio lessons and conduct the reinforcing activities after the radio lesson. In general, however, it is best to keep change to the minimum necessary, making it more likely that teachers will use radio programmes effectively.

Given the complexity of the management task, management training for administrative staff can be extremely valuable. Microcomputers can help staff manage the project more effectively. They can be useful in evaluating impact, compiling results in a way that decision-makers can understand, and helping develop support for education radio programmes.

Technical Requirements
In addition to the technical requirements discussed above for all educational technologies, including power sources and equipment maintenance, radio has certain special requirements. There must be access to radio transmission facilities during times appropriate for classroom lessons, and at a reasonable cost. It is also necessary to ensure that transmission signals are clear to all schools receiving the programmes.

Many developing countries are building new studios to produce instructional programming, while renting transmission time from national public networks for broadcasting. In a few countries, education radio projects have complete, independent facilities. Thailand, for example, has developed a new radio transmission system dedicated solely to educational programming.

Where commercial stations must be rented and there are scheduling problems, it may be worthwhile to distribute tape recorders to schools so that teachers can record programmes during broadcasting and replay them at appropriate times during the school day.

Opportunities in the Coming Decade

Despite its success, particularly at the primary education level, radio has not been fully utilized to deliver education or training on a national scale (except for Thailand's primary education radio programme). In some countries, despite the positive impact demonstrated by radio education and training projects, they have been abandoned.

During the coming decade, this medium should be exploited far more fully. It will be necessary, therefore, to conduct research that answers some key questions. Why is radio not used more widely to deliver education and training? Is it a matter of attitudes toward education technology? Are signals too unreliable? Are recurrent costs of radio too high? Is the effort to integrate radio into ongoing instruction too difficult?

Other policy issues will also have to be addressed in the coming decade if the potential of education radio is to be fully realized. One set of questions concerns centralization vs. local relevance. To what extent can a country use a centralized curriculum successfully? How can a curriculum be "tailored" to local conditions and culture? What is the best way to ensure satisfactory broadcast quality at the local level? Can local broadcasting expand access and improve relevance? Where there is local resistance to using education radio, how is it best addressed?

Finally, prototypes of successful programmes must be developed. To do so, it will be necessary to determine the factors that make some programmes successful, and the features that model programmes should contain in order to be effective across countries. Developing such models will not only help establish high-quality education and training programmes, but will also reduce development costs since adaptation is far less expensive than original development.

5.3 Radiovision and Tape-Slide

Radiovision and tape-slide presentations are very similar. Radiovision combines slides with lectures taped from radio. Although it has not been adopted nearly as widely as radio broadcast programmes, it is a very powerful combination, providing all the benefits of education radio, plus visuals. It thus has most of the features of TV, except motion.

Synchronized tape-slide presentations combine pre-taped lectures with slides. Like radiovision, synchronized tape-slide presentations offer a number of advantages. They provide a combination of audio and visual information. They provide consistent quality of instruction. Material can be presented in realistic detail, raising student interest and involvement. They can be used by learners of varying ages and do not require literacy. The technologies are flexible and can be fitted to individual class schedules. In addition, they allow students to work at their own pace.

Unlike radiovision, which is best used for relatively large groups of learners, tape-slide presentations can provide specialized instruction for small groups, making it particularly appropriate for vocational training. Although audio instruction alone would rarely be sufficient to teach technical content, along with slides and worksheets or manuals it can be highly effective.

Materials for tape-slide are relatively easy to develop and can be produced by developing country educational institutions. When materials become obsolete, they can easily be replaced or revised—a feature particularly important for vocational training. The ease with which tape-slide presentations can be tailored to local situations and languages is valuable for general education, and is especially important for vocational training. A great deal of tape-slide courseware, both for general education and vocational education, is available either inexpensively or free and can be easily adapted. The equipment for both radiovision and tape-slide presentations is simple to operate, portable, durable, and inexpensive in comparison with video.

There is little research on radiovision impacts. Most research on tape-slide instruction suggests, however, that it generally produces learning gains at least equal to conventional teaching. These results apply both to academic subjects and to vocational training.

In some subject areas, tape-slide instruction appears to be more effective than conventional teaching. In a study of science laboratory instruction, for example, students using tape-slide instruction outperformed students receiving conventional instruction. In a study of para-professional self-instruction, students using tape-slides performed significantly better on tests than a group using videocassettes. Studies also suggest that tape-slides are even more effective when combined with worksheets or manuals (Sharma, pp. 9-13).

Thus, it appears that tape-slide and radiovision can be extremely valuable education technologies in areas where qualified teachers are not available. They are also effective in improving the quality of conventional instruction and in providing review. Unlike broadcast radio, however, radiovision and tape-slides, or simply audiotape recorders alone, are not widely used in schools in developing countries.

Pedagogical Requirements
The requirements of radiovision and tape-slide technology are much like those of radio. Materials must fit the curriculum and instructional style of the schools, student and teacher skills and the culture and values of users. The quality of the instruction and the impact will depend on the quality of content and instructional design. Because there is a large quantity of materials available, countries can choose material that fits their systems, and make necessary adaptations relatively easily.

Financial Requirements
Although radiovision and tape-slide technology are relatively inexpensive, they are more costly than radio alone. Audiocassette recorders and slide projectors must be acquired. Tapes, slides, and any associated materials must be purchased. Although most of the equipment is quite durable, tapes are more fragile and must be replaced after some time. Maintenance is more expensive than for radio, in part because servicing for radio is more widely available and partly because there is more equipment to maintain.

Management Requirements
The management requirements for radiovision and tape-slide are much like those for radio. Teachers must be trained to use the

technology effectively and be given incentives—tangible or intangible—to integrate it into their instruction.

Careful management will be necessary to use radiovision or tape-slide effectively in a developing country. Content expertise, skills in instructional design, and technical skills in photography and audio recording must be brought together and managed effectively.

In order to take advantage of the wealth of materials that exists, education authorities must have access to information sources about the availability of tape-slide presentations. Directories like *Words on Tape* can be helpful in this regard.

In many cases, developing countries will themselves have to evaluate the tape-slide presentations in order to identify those appropriate to their education or training curriculum. It will also be important to establish two-way communication between instructors and central education authorities so that policy makers can get feedback on the radiovision and tape-slide presentations that are most effective for general education and vocational training in different circumstances.

Technical Requirements

The most important special technical requirement for using radiovision or tape-slide presentations is the provision of training in the use and maintenance of the equipment, slides and tapes.

Opportunities in the Coming Decade

In the coming decade, radiovision can be used far more widely and effectively than it is being used today. One obstacle that can be overcome relatively easily involves technical issues, i.e., problems in getting and using tape recorders and visuals. Thus, it will be useful to build small, portable "kits" that include all of the necessary equipment for radiovision, including tape recorder, radio receiver, and slide projector (Sharma, 1988).

Although tape-slide technology appears to offer a number of advantages, it is little used in schools in developing countries. Before it will be more widely adopted, research is likely to be necessary to determine the reasons it is not now used.

It is unlikely that radiovision or tape-slide presentations will become as widely used as interactive radio in the coming decade.

The use of radiovision and tape-slides may increase, however, as a method of enhancing the quality, and increasing the flexibility, of broadcast radio courses.

5.4 Television

Education television (ETV), defined here as broadcast television specifically designed to be part of a general education or vocational training curriculum, can be a powerful medium of instruction. It can deliver vivid instruction in high level skill areas that require both audio and visual channels. In science courses, for example, it can guide students through complicated or dangerous experiments. In training, it can show the use of machinery not otherwise available and guide students through complicated or dangerous operations. With Video Cassette Recorders (VCRs), the instruction can be made available at a time convenient for learners and instructors.

There are serious drawbacks, however. All this power is expensive, both in financial resources and human skills. It is a price few developing countries can afford. Many education professionals, even in developed countries, believe the expense of education television far outweighs its contributions. It also seems to engender more teacher resistance than other education technologies.

The cost issues are particularly restrictive for using television for vocational training. All forms for instructional television, including cable, closed circuit, open transmission, microwave, and satellite, require high use levels to justify cost. In most developing countries, there is rarely a training group large enough to warrant the costs of television.

ETV can be used, however, to provide large groups of viewers with information on such general subjects as labor market data, career requirements, and training opportunities. It has also been used successfully to inform farmers of improved agricultural techniques and to train agriculture extension workers in Africa. In Ivory Coast, for example, a programme to raise rice production used television in combination with other media and extension workers to teach improved rice farming techniques. The programme raised rice production significantly, and television was credited with contributing substantially to the positive impact. Yet television alone is not very effective in teaching farmers new agricultural techniques. It is best used to support other media and extension services.

The quality of televised agricultural programmes, and their ability to "speak to" the average farmer, determines their effectiveness. Boring lectures or highly sophisticated discussions have little impact. Agricultural programmes are most effective when they show farmers and use language farmers understand.

Impact on Achievement

The impact of education television has been mixed. At the primary level, ETV has largely failed to make a contribution worth the costs. At the post-primary level, there are several success stories. Mexico's Telesecundaria System, for example, has made secondary education available to many who would otherwise not have access to it. Achievement gains have been approximately equivalent to conventional secondary schools, at costs less than those of conventional schools. The disparities between achievement of rural and urban ETV students has been less than that which usually exists in conventional secondary schools. The system has been accepted by teachers and other education professionals; by the end of this decade, it may reach one million students.

China has been successfully taking advantage of ETV to deliver university education. The Central Radio and TV University (CRTVU), under the Ministry of Broadcasting and Ministry of Education, produces programmes for broadcast, as well as audiocassettes of particular courses. Students are between the ages of 18 and 35, most are employed, about half are skilled, and about 38 per cent are underqualified teachers. Achievements of CRTVU are notable. Of 110,000 students registered in 1979, 78,000 (69 per cent) received degrees in 1982.

CRTVU plans to expand courses and students. Many new courses will be directly vocational, determined by national and local needs. Wherever possible, CRTVU plans to use existing polytechnical curricula to design the courses.

Nonetheless, the programme is not without problems. Although its university courses are supposed to be the equivalent of conventional college, CRTVU students cannot apply to conventional universities or other institutions of higher education. They rarely get salary rates equivalent to those who attend regular college.

Despite success stories like these, ETV has had little impact in improving education and training in most developing countries. It has been argued that ETV is no more effective than conventional instruction, and is more expensive.

Consider the ETV programme in El Salvador, which was used to expand access to the 7th-9th grades. The impact was mixed—in some areas ETV students excelled in comparison with other students; in other areas they did not do as well. The programme also generated strong teacher opposition.

Even where the impact appeared to be positive, ETV programmes have been cancelled; the reasons are unclear, though probably largely political. The recent trend has been to move TVs out of formal education facilities and into community centers. Ivory Coast is a good example. The Government had developed a large ETV programme in the 1970s, with 20,000 government-owned TVs throughout the country. The ETV programme helped raise educational opportunities in rural areas and reduce repetition and dropout rates. The cost per graduate was less than that of conventional schools. Nevertheless, it has been abandoned. Recently the televisions have been removed from schools and placed in village community centers.

Pedagogical Requirements

The general pedagogical principles of education technologies apply equally to ETV. Educational goals must be clear and acceptable to teachers. Content and instructional design must be of high quality, relevant to students' experience and culture, and delivered in a language students understand. This is particularly important—and difficult—in countries where programmes are developed at the center for culturally diverse communities.

In addition, television offers a panoply of techniques for actively engaging viewers. Yet the potential of TV often remains unexploited, and education and training programmes are tedious and boring. In most countries, ETV programmes need to be made more effective and engaging. To make material more relevant for local viewers, shooting in the rural areas can be effective. In addition, women, who often constitute a large part of farm labor—up to 80 per cent in Africa—should not be ignored in agricultural programming.

Financial Requirements
Education television is expensive. Initial investment costs, maintenance and production costs are high. The medium requires an audience in the hundreds of thousands, and use over a relatively long period (perhaps 20 years), in order to be cost-effective. The financial expense is raised if VCRs are used—probably keeping that technology out of reach for most developing countries in the coming decade.

Yet it is worth noting that some programmes have been cost-effective. The Ivory Coast television project cost approximately $13 per student per year—less that the cost of conventional schooling (based on 336,000 students). Studies of the Mexico Telesecundaria system show costs to be equal to or about 25 per cent lower than conventional secondary schools. The lower figures were attributable to lower costs for physical facilities, lower salaries and lower administrative costs. Korea's Air and Correspondence University has an average cost one tenth that of conventional universities. Pakistan's Allama Eqbal Open University is about half the cost of conventional universities. Thailand's Sukhothai Thammathirat Open University is less than one fifth the cost of conventional universities. It is important to note that for primary education, where a teacher is necessary, the cost figures would be different, and ETV undoubtedly not cost-effective.

Although ETV is now out of reach of most developing country budgets, expenses are dropping. Equipment is getting lighter, cheaper, and easier to use. The costs of satellite transmission are declining. While still expensive, satellite channels can cover thousands of square miles, making it possible to get information to large numbers of people. Similarly, the cost of special technologies like VCRs, solar-powered sets, portable equipment, and large-screen TV sets are dropping.

Management Requirements
Education television involves all of the management issues associated with other educational technologies: leadership, people, management systems, structure. For TV, however, these issues are more complex and difficult to handle. Leadership must therefore be stronger. The development of human skills becomes more complicated and challenging. For management staff itself,

management training is critical to enabling them to do their jobs effectively.

Other kinds of training also become more critical. Training in curriculum design and programme production are essential. Skilled personnel who have more experience producing interesting programmes need to be recruited or developed. Currently, in most developing countries there are few professionals, and they are poorly trained. As a result, many productions use boring "talking heads" formats. Similarly, training in equipment maintenance is much more complicated and less available than is the case with radio.

The issue of structure and its complexity with regard to ETV is made abundantly clear by the Satellite Instructional TV Experiment in India. Because television studios are expensive and skilled personnel are rare, programmes were developed in a centralized fashion. Yet the audience is culturally highly diverse, and many programmes did not fit viewer culture and language. It will be rare that a developing country will be able to afford the resources necessary to develop and test ETV models in culturally different communities to see where different models work best.

Technical Requirements
Human technical skills in video production are a major constraint to effective ETV. Although equipment is becoming simpler, it is still complex and difficult to use. In addition, for an ETV programme to be cost-effective, it must use TV stations large and powerful enough to send signals to a very large audience. At the viewer site, there must be receivers, maintenance services, access to spare parts, and an adequate power supply. Receivers must be "tropicalized" for many climates. If VCRs are used, they add to expense as well as technical complexity.

Opportunities in the Coming Decade
The controversy over the value and expense of ETV continues to be heated. Critics argue that ETV takes more than its fair share of education technology budgets, leaving too little to develop other technologies, such as radio, and without producing valuable impact. Yet some developing countries have used ETV in a powerful and cost-effective manner. They demonstrate that under the right circumstances, and with the right kinds of programming, ETV can be a valuable asset to an education or training system.

The coming decade may well be a turning point for the use of education television in developing countries. During this period, countries will either withdraw much of the funding that has gone into ETV and allocate it elsewhere, or educators will identify the conditions in which ETV is valuable and the qualities of programming that make it cost-effective, making ETV much stronger.

Despite criticism, the spread of television in developing countries makes it unlikely that ETV will be ignored completely in the coming decade. In Africa (excluding the Arab states), for example, between 1960 and 1976, TV sets, which now number several million, increased 20 times. This trend is likely to continue in most developing countries.

The rise in adoption of TV sets will provide opportunities to use ETV to reach large numbers of people with instruction they would otherwise never receive. Furthermore, television has the ability to capture people's attention; it will be unfortunate if the medium is not exploited to improve education and training.

In order to do so, however, developing countries need to get more information about successful ETV programmes. Research is needed to identify the conditions under which ETV is appropriate and the "success factors" for ETV under various circumstances. In addition, ETV programming models need to be developed and tested to bring about improvement in programme quality.

Cost-effective ways of creating good quality ETV programming must also be explored. For example, ETV staff can utilize the large film libraries of organizations like UNICEF, WHO, and UNESCO, and adapt them to meet local education needs. Finally, countries will need access to information about technological innovations that significantly improve instruction power while reducing costs.

5.5 Teleconferencing

Like radio and television, teleconferencing offers a means of delivering instruction to large numbers of learners who otherwise would not have access to that level and quality of instruction. The unique contribution of teleconferencing is immediate interaction between instructors and students who are separated by distance. It is the desirability of such immediate interaction that justifies the cost of a teleconferencing system.

Although there are several types of telecommunications systems used for teleconferencing, satellite systems are the most promising. With satellites ringing the globe, it is now possible to link virtually anyplace on earth to a telecommunications network. Satellite systems are increasingly being used in developing countries to deliver scarce education and training instruction to distant, multiple sites, with two-way communications systems that allow learners to ask questions of the instructor. This two-way interaction, when effectively built into the design of the instruction, contributes greatly to learning. The systems also facilitate education management with two-way communication between participating organizations and central government agency offices.

Teleconferencing via satellite is a highly flexible technology. It has been used successfully to deliver university courses, in-service training, health campaign co-ordination, medical consultation assistance, and management conferences.

During the last thirty years, the technology has made tremendous advances. Satellites are becoming more powerful, requiring smaller receiving stations and greatly reducing the cost of the system. The satellites themselves rarely pose reliability problems, and earth station technology is increasingly reliable (Distance Education). India, Indonesia, Brazil, Mexico, China, and a coalition of 22 Arab states have launched their own satellites. Through Intelsat, 27 other developing countries have telecommunications systems based on satellite.

Extending Education and Training via Teleconferencing
Teleconferencing has been used in several developing countries to expand access to higher education and in-service training. Results have been quite promising. One of the best cited efforts is the USAID Rural Satellite Program (RSP), established in 1980. The RSP created three pilot projects to determine how well a relatively simple, inexpensive, interactive satellite-based telephone system could expand education and technical training opportunities in rural and remote areas.

The three pilot projects, in Indonesia, Peru, and the West Indies, linked remote universities and professional agencies with one another and national centers of expertise, making it possible to provide teleconferencing for multi-site conferences and classes. The networks use commercial satellite channels for long-distance transmission, and a combination of local earth stations, land wires, microwave, and radio to connect local sites.

Although, where available, face-to-face quality instruction is still preferable, the projects showed that teleconferencing can have impressive results. They demonstrated that teleconferencing can provide a cost-effective means for delivering high-quality instruction to universities and working professionals in remote or rural areas. Acceptance by instructors and students has been extremely positive. In the Indonesian system, for example, 67 per cent of students and 95 per cent of local tutors reported that teleconferencing instruction was equally or more effective than regular courses. They also indicated the value of two-way interaction between instructor and learner—74 per cent of students said they learned from the question and discussion periods.

The West Indies teleconferencing system (UWIDITE) primarily serves small groups of adults in isolated areas who want training in their area of professional interest. Again, student response has been highly positive, with 68 per cent reporting that they learned as much or more from the telecommunications classes as from conventional classes and 89 per cent saying that classes are interesting.

Similarly, Peru's PCSP provides audio-conferences primarily for in-service training. More than 92 per cent of the audio-conference participants in the programmes reported that the programme improved their skills and job performance. More than half said that the system had provided essential information and training they could not otherwise have received. In 1985, the system delivered more than 300 teleconferences at field workers' request. The success of the pilot has convinced the Government of Peru to make telecommunications a priority investment for rural areas.

The projects are also cost-effective. The Indonesian project is indicative. It provides expert instruction, instruction materials, and in-service training for local lecturers for about half the cost of conventional universities. The systems also substitute for bringing people together physically for training, resulting in considerable savings. For example, a one-week seminar for 30 people in the Caribbean would cost about $19,000, in contrast to the marginal cost of $6,000 to deliver the same training via teleconferencing.

Pedagogical Requirements

As with any education technology, content and instructional design are key. Topics must be interesting. Qualified instructors must be willing to teach over this medium. The quality of the pedagogical approach is key, because it determines system design choices, e.g., providing audiovisual or only audio communication and the features of interactivity.

It is also important to have lecturers, tutors, or other less senior teaching staff present at each class. These teachers should help students adjust to the technology, motivate students to attend all classes and provide backup discussions that support learning from the lectures.

Financial Requirements

The costs of teleconferencing systems vary widely, depending on the type and capacity of the system. One fundamental factor determining cost is whether the system provides audio and/or video. Although video adds interest and visual information, it also raises costs considerably.

The choice between audio and audiovisual affects the five major cost factors of the system. First is materials preparation. Audiovisual production is much more expensive than simple audio production. Second, the satellite transmitter costs vary since the band width for video is approximately 1,500 times that of voice. As a result, video transmission is much more expensive, perhaps twice as much as voice. Third is the space portion of the system. Again video is much more expensive than voice, although it may be possible to share this expense with commercial or other public sector users. Fourth, satellite receivers are more expensive for video. Although the difference is not great in absolute terms for one receiver, the total expense is high because a number of receivers are needed. Fifth, a television, loudspeaker, or other device is needed in the classroom. Again the numbers drive up the expense.

It is worth noting that all costs other than the first and fifth are fungible, i.e., can be used for other purposes to defray costs. Thus, several agencies could share the costs of the infrastructure. The Ministry of Education, for example, could transmit university programmes during the day, the Ministry of Agriculture could transmit weather or agricultural marketing information in the evening.

The design of the system, e.g., whether it will be one-way or two-way, and the type of two-way system, and whether it will use satellite, microwave, cable, etc. all influence costs. Whatever the system, it will be essential to build ongoing maintenance into any funding scheme. The system will need regular servicing as well as at least occasional repair, and funds must be available to acquire these services.

Although costs will vary widely among countries and different types and capacities of systems, it is interesting to note that all of the RSP systems were less expensive per course than physically bringing instructors to participating universities or bringing individuals together for a seminar.

It is also worth noting that the Peru RSP system suggests that:

> ...rural telecommunications systems do generate healthy revenues. It is possible that they can cover operating costs and, with careful pricing, even defray start-up costs. From a development perspective, rural communications systems are unique. Few other development investments generate revenues and are eagerly paid for by users. Road systems do not; sanitation systems do not. (Tietjen, 1987)

Management Requirements

The most important management requirement is to understand that teleconferencing is a system and must be managed as one. The system needs a "champion" at the center of government, i.e., a leader with power and access to resources who will ensure the system gets the resources its needs. It also needs a strong project leader who can communicate effectively with the central government about project successes and needs.

The teleconferencing system's structure, and the complexity of managing it, will vary with such factors as capacity, system configuration, types of equipment used, and the political and organizational characteristics of participating organizations. Whatever the structure, the institution responsible for overall system management must be strong enough to access resources and personnel needed to make the system successful and have enough authority over local sites to keep day-to-day management smooth. It is also critical that all participating institutions, including the Public Telephone and Telegraph Company, see how they can benefit from the system, develop a sense of "ownership" in the system, and identify a "champion" in the organization who can support the system effectively.

Training will be necessary for many diverse groups. Upper level decision makers and planners in education will have to become familiar with the capabilities of the system and its requirements. Faculty may need assistance designing and delivering programmes that are appropriate for the system and for the conditions of all participating institutions. Students will need help in using the system effectively.

Telecommunications staff will need training in new technologies and management procedures to operate and maintain a satellite-based teleconferencing system. This may include overseas training, teleconferencing in-service training, on-the-job hands-on training, and printed materials, e.g., manuals.

Technical Requirements

One of the most important technical requirements is an accurate baseline assessment of existing resources, including local telecommunications lines. Using existing telecommunications facilities as much as possible can help keep costs down—but only if the lines can be made to carry a reliable signal without undue "noise." Reliability problems in a satellite system are usually due to local telephone lines. The next most likely area of problem is in the end-receiving equipment, e.g., loudspeakers or televisions.

The technical requirements are so varied, depending on the system, and so complex, it is only feasible here to point out some pitfalls to avoid. First, in an audio-conferencing system, audio equipment is far more important than supplemental equipment such as telewriters (to transmit live writing or text) or slow-scan video (to transfer pictures or print). These latter types of equipment are not only expensive, but often have problems, and may not operate at all in the developing country telecommunications environment. If this type of equipment is going to be used, it is essential that it be field tested before massive purchases are made. Although instructors may insist that graphics capacity is necessary, the RSP projects suggest that it is often not essential, particularly if good instruction materials are distributed before classes.

Second, it is important to start simple and increase complexity of equipment if staff, time, finances and skills can support it. If non-technical people will operate equipment, it must be kept simple enough for them to use. It is safer to use few channels and depend on narrow-bank technologies that use single telephone lines, rather than broad-band technologies like television that use the equivalent of 600 telephone circuits. It is also best to use simple, commercially available equipment rather than any unique prototype equipment. In addition, it is worth noting that pilot-testing two-site linkages may not reveal the way multi-site linkages will operate—the latter being far more difficult to operate to ensure signals free of noise.

Power is also necessary, although the amount of power required for receivers is quite low. It may be possible to run the receivers with batteries that are rechargeable by solar power. In Indonesia, for example, a satellite earth station and audio-conferencing equipment used photovoltaics and ran on approximately the power that operates a home steam iron.

Comprehensive and reliable maintenance facilities are needed, as well as a regular maintenance plan. One rule of thumb is that 10 per cent of the total value of equipment should be budgeted for maintenance.

Opportunities in the Coming Decade
In the coming decade, teleconferencing—either audio or audiovisual—will offer a powerful medium for bringing high-quality university instruction or professional training to rural and remote areas. Although not as attractive to students as face-to-face instruction, it will provide a good alternative where in-person instruction is otherwise unavailable. In combination with radio, teleconferencing will be able to offer instruction very widely, along with the opportunity for listeners to call in questions on the teleconferencing system—all at a relatively low cost. The technology will be most appropriate for teaching adults, who are able to work largely independently.

Audio-conferencing has already proven cost-effective under various conditions and costs of basic equipment are likely to continue to drop. At the same time, service quality will increase, with greater access to satellite channels and expanded capability including integrated voice, video and data-text services at reasonable costs. With the latter will come easier and cheaper ways to distribute supplementary printed instructional materials. In addition, equipment will become more power-efficient and photovoltaic cells are likely to be an inexpensive source of sufficient power in many countries.

Many of the sophisticated graphics equipment, e.g., telewriters, and the receiving units, e.g., televisions, are now the least reliable parts of the system. During the coming decade, they are likely to become cheaper, sturdier, and easier to use and maintain. These changes, along with reduction in the level of costs of the system as a whole, will give developing countries more options for delivering instruction. They will also demand more skilled professionals to fully exploit the capabilities of the more sophisticated equipment. The result can be wide dissemination of high-quality post-secondary education and training.

This is also a technology that calls for good co-ordination and co-operation among different government agencies, particularly if agencies want to share a satellite channel. In the coming decade, countries can have commercial users share teleconferencing systems with education and training programmes in order to generate revenues that cover the costs of those programmes. For example, a telecommunications system can provide vocational training to employees of scattered businesses for a fee. A telecommunications system can offer commercial telephone service in addition to education and training teleconferencing. Demand for telephone service in the coming decade, even in rural areas, may well defray the costs of the entire system.

Similarly, developing countries can share satellite channels and the development of educational and training programmes. Through teleconferencing, they can exchange information and experience, support one another more effectively, and have less one-way dependence on the industrialized countries.

5.6 Computers

The issues regarding computers in education are even more complex and controversial than those of other technologies. It is beyond the scope of this paper to address all of the facets of those issues. What we will do here is examine some of the contributions computers have made in developing country education and training systems, and the requirements and opportunities revealed by those experiences.

Two types of computer hardware are generally used in education and vocational training programmes: minicomputers and microcomputers. Although the line between them is rapidly blurring, minicomputers are more powerful, with a single computer and several terminals on which people can work. They are usually accompanied by a complete, integrated curriculum package, typically having features for evaluating and monitoring students.

Microcomputers are somewhat less powerful than minis, although they can have considerable power. Microcomputers can be "stand-alone," running software independently, or networked to share software. They are less expensive than minicomputers, and more flexible, having a greater variety of software available.

Software is extremely varied and of uneven quality, particularly for microcomputers. Some of the most common programmes are:

- drill and practice, which uses repetition to help students consolidate skills, without introducing any new learning material;
- tutorials, which provide instruction in new materials, geared to the learning style and skills of the user;
- simulations, which portray models of "real-life" situations, using limited parameters, so that students can apply skills to solve life-like problems;
- programming languages, which students can use to build codes that control computer operations to a greater or lesser extent;
- personal productivity tools, which are content-free packages used for a function, e.g., word processing, and;
- computer-managed instruction, which can help teachers evaluate student skills, diagnose difficulties, prescribe instruction, monitor progress, and create reports.

Whether or not computers are "appropriate" for the education systems of developing countries, they have been embraced by many as crucial. A statement by UNESCO expresses the feelings of many education policy makers in developing countries:

UNESCO holds with the principle that informatics for educational purposes should be considered from the point of view of the democratization of education and equality of opportunity for all. An unequal development of informatics would widen the gap between developed and developing countries. The risk of disparity exists not only as between countries, however, but also within each country if the development of informatics means advantaging a minority of the population at the expense of its majority (UNESCO in Prospects, Vol XVII, No. 3, 1987 (63), p. 327).

How can computers help to improve education? There are four areas in which computers can be of value: management of education systems; computer-aided instruction; personal productivity tools, and; development of programming skills.

Management of Education Systems
This may be where the most apparent contribution lies. Micro or minicomputers can be used to improve planning and budget functions, help assess educational programmes, monitor activities, and support administrative activities. They can also be used to integrate, co-ordinate, guide and evaluate student learning, reducing record keeping and supplying a wide range of information to instructors.

Computers can be extremely valuable for vocational education planning and management, which require many types of analysis, including analysis of manpower data, demographic data, cost and finance data of training programmes. Computers can help link analysis to action by permitting analysis to be conducted quickly enough so that findings can be applied to ongoing policy and management decisions. Furthermore, planning and curriculum decisions are often best done at the local level, involving the private sector and community leaders and linking training to the needs of indigenous businesses (Herschbach). Computers, particularly microcomputers, can help local planners and decision-makers conduct information-based decision-making.

Computer-Aided Instruction
Most of the controversy about computers in education focuses on

computer-aided instruction (CAI). Some argue that CAI helps students learn better and faster, and can stimulate cognitive development. Others hold that there is little or no positive impact, despite the great cost. There are five situations in which CAI is clearly worth considering as a cost-effective teaching method:

- programmes with very high teacher/student ratios, where computers can substitute for some teaching staff;
- programmes that have no qualified teachers in some area in which computers can provide instruction;
- programmes for special needs learners, either highly gifted or slow learners, who can work alone with the computer;
- adult learning situations when it is difficult to schedule regular classes, and the adults can work independently with the computer; and
- general education or vocational training courses in which computer tutorial or simulation programmes can substitute for expensive laboratories or other equipment, or dangerous experiments.

In general, however, CAI has not been used in those situations. Instead, it is adopted by conventional schools to boost student skills in basic mathematics, languages, and the sciences. The cost-effectiveness of computers for these kinds of uses is far more questionable.

Most of the evidence and experience with computers in education—primarily microcomputers—has been gathered in the developed countries. In the U.S., microcomputers are proliferating rapidly in schools. Recent statistics show that 95 per cent of all public schools have at least one computer, with a computer/student ratio of 1:32. Five sixths of primary schools have a computer for instruction, with the average computer/student ratio approximately 1:40 (and vast differences among schools). A majority of secondary schools have 15 or more computers for instruction. Typically, students have limited use of the machines—about half an hour a week.

How are these computers used? In primary schools, about three quarters of the time on the computer is used for drill and practice in reading, language arts and arithmetic. There is much controversy about their cost-effectiveness as a substitute for teachers in this function. Nonetheless, interest in introducing primary school children to computer use is strong, and the number of microcomputers is likely to continue to increase in primary schools, particularly in wealthier schools.

In secondary schools, about 40 per cent of the time on the computer is used to teach programming. Students also use computers as personal productivity tools, with spreadsheets, word processing and data base management.

Proponents of CAI argue that computers offer important advantages in teaching. They provide students with immediate feedback. They can individualize instruction for the user. They are interesting and versatile, stimulating student involvement and motivating learning.

Some studies in the U.S. have supported this view, showing fairly strong positive impacts on student achievement, e.g., effect sizes in primary school of .47-.53 (Anzalone, p. 46). Studies also show, however, that certain "soft" education technologies are more effective than CAI. For example, peer tutoring, in which students tutor those who are younger, has been shown to be more cost-effective than CAI in teaching reading and mathematics. Peer tutoring is also labor intensive, and fits the cultures of many developing countries.

On the other hand, CAI appears to be more cost-effective than some other methods of improving student achievement, including reducing class size, increasing instructional time, and adult tutoring. (Adult tutoring, while extremely effective, is also very expensive.) Despite the cost-effectiveness calculations, however, the introduction of computers has rarely reduced costs per pupil. Rather, computers tend to become an added cost to conventional instruction.

The U.S. is not alone in adopting computers in education. Many countries, including Australia, Canada, France, Hungary, Korea, Mexico, Spain, Japan, and the U.K. have general policies to introduce microcomputers into primary and secondary schools. In Japan, for example, 81 per cent of public vocational schools, 78 per cent or private vocational schools, and about half of general secondary schools use computers for training and instruction. "Experiments" in introducing computers into schools are being conducted in many developing countries, including Argentina, Brazil, China, Colombia, Kenya and Senegal.

The goal of many of these programmes is "computer

literacy," a phrase without a precise meaning. It is usually used to describe the process of getting people comfortable with using a computer, although it can also mean giving people skills in programming or in the use of personal productivity tools. As is reflected in the UNESCO statement above, many people believe that computers will be a permanent, and prominent, feature of the future workworld and that it is imperative for students to learn to use the machines.

Computers in higher education are more familiar and less controversial. Large universities have been using mainframe computers for decades. Microcomputers now deliver many of the same functions, along with substantial power, at much lower cost. As a result, computers have become accessible even to many smaller, poorer universities. They are most widely used as a management tool. Less often, they are used for instruction, e.g., for personal productivity tools, programming and simulation. In addition, they can connect to national or international networks in order to access data or communicate with distant organizations.

Programming and Personal Productivity Tools

Programming is taught primarily at secondary and post-secondary levels. The intent is twofold: (1) to strengthen higher order cognitive skills, such as logic, and generalizable problem-solving skills such as planning, and; (2) to develop a practical skill that will serve the student in the workplace.

There has been substantial criticism of programming courses in general education. Some believe that poorly designed and taught programming courses have discouraged students from entering computer science fields. They argue that a more effective way to teach students to use computers is by introducing them to personal productivity tools. For example, students can learn to use word processing to compose papers, or data base management to analyze data. In addition, studies indicate that girls and boys enjoy courses using personal productivity tools about equally, while girls enjoy programming courses far less than boys do (Lockheed).

A major problem with this approach is that there is little curricula designed to integrate computer use into general education instruction. Teachers do not know how to integrate computers into their instruction themselves. Furthermore, computers are often kept in one "computer room," making it difficult to arrange for students to do coursework using the computers.

Despite these obstacles, it may be valuable for computer courses to teach students to use personal productivity tools independently of content. Studies show that students prefer learning to use those tools to learning programming, and their attitudes toward computer use are more positive than when they are given programming courses (Lockheed). Furthermore, in the process of using computers to learn other subjects, students are also learning skills that can be transferred to work.

In contrast to primary and general secondary schools, vocational/technical schools, universities, and specialized training organizations have experienced significant savings through their use of computers in training. Computers have cut the costs of direct supervision and have been used for simulation of expensive machinery (Oliviera). A major obstacle to wider use has been the limited number of firms marketing specifically vocational training software packages.

It is impossible to discuss all of the requirements for a successful adoption of computers into an educational system because they vary greatly depending on the purpose of adoption and the circumstances of the system. Nonetheless, some requirements are critical for all computer adoption efforts, and we discuss them briefly. It is important to note that these requirements are interdependent—to be successful, computer adoption must fulfill all of the requirements.

Pedagogical Requirements

Three pedagogical requirements are key to effective use of computers in education: linking computer adoption to educational goals; acquiring high-quality and appropriate software, and; fostering equity between sexes and ethnic groups.

It is all too easy to assume that computers can solve educational problems that are rooted in fundamental conditions in the education system and society, but such assumptions are dangerous. It is essential to recognize that computers are only a tool. They must be introduced and used to support clear educational goals, otherwise they can create, rather than solve, problems by absorbing scarce funds for equipment that is not used, misdirecting staff time, and exacerbating inequality in education.

The first step in adopting a computer system is to determine the educational objectives which a computer is expected to help achieve. The next step is to choose software that will support achievement of those goals. Hardware can then be chosen to run the software. Software must fit the students' language and culture, as well as the curriculum of the school. Currently, most developing countries import software from developed countries, and are likely to continue to do so. Problems arise if the software is not culturally appropriate, since most software is difficult to adapt.

The pedagogical requirements in computer training will vary depending on the goals of specific countries. Some quite advanced countries will want to develop a wide spectrum of training programmes, from those producing highly sophisticated programmers to those teaching the use of personal productivity tools. Other countries may want to develop certain computer-related specialties requiring focused training. Still others may want to develop end-user ability and skills in computer maintenance. Training programmes thus must respond to the economic and skill needs of particular countries and areas within countries.

One difficulty developing countries face is in evaluating software before purchasing it. The U.S. has approximately 20,000 educational software programmes on the market. Only about 10 per cent of those have been formally evaluated. Even acquiring evaluation information about those programmes is not an easy task for educators in developing countries.

A special challenge in teaching students to use computers is to encourage equity between sexes and ethnic groups. One method that has proven highly effective is to create "computer tutors." These students work with others of the same sex and ethnic group to help them learn to use the computer and overcome problems. When tutees learn computer skills, they in turn become tutors.

There are some particular constraints to using computers cost-effectively for vocational education. One problem in teaching vocational computer skills is that hardware and software are rapidly changing, making it difficult and expensive to keep curricula and instructor knowledge current. Another difficulty is the lack of software specifically designed for vocational training. The tutorial and drill-and-practice software that dominates educational software has limited use for vocational and technical instruction (Herschbach).

It is also argued by vocational education specialists that teaching professional computer skills requires a professional computer science teacher; in-service training of a non-computer science teacher will not be sufficient. Teaching personal productivity tools to those who will use them at work can be done by non-computer science teachers who have learned to use the computer (Herschbach).

Vocational training in computer skills should be "hands-on" and reflect labour market demand. Students can learn to use programming languages that are relatively standard worldwide. The computer skills which will most be in demand in the coming decade, however, will be skills in using personal productivity tools, not programming skills. There are several fairly standard personal productivity tools used in the U.S. and Europe. Learning word processing, business applications, and job-related applications of database management using such packages can be highly valuable. It is worth noting, however, that often these skills can be learned relatively briefly on the job.

Financial Requirements
The costs of computers in education vary greatly among developing countries. For many, however, costs per student per hour for direct computer use are more than all other education costs per student per week.

Any educational institution considering purchasing a computer system must take into account all of the elements necessary to get the computer system up and running and keep it operating effectively: hardware—purchase and maintenance; software—purchase and updating; training; transferring records from paper to disk; peripherals, e.g., printer, modem; facilities (especially if special facilities are required), and; power consumption.

The price of hardware fell 50 per cent between 1980 and 1986, and will continue to decline in the coming decade. Yet hardware is only about 11 per cent of the cost of CAI. Thus, if other costs stay the same—or even rise, as they are likely to do—the drop in hardware costs will have little impact. In addition, this cost distribution makes it clear that even if computers are donated, they are not a "free good." The education system must make all of the related investments in order to use the computers effectively.

One of the most time-consuming and underestimated financial requirements is for record transfer of data from existing paper files to the computer. This process often demands a considerable investment of personnel time in order to arrange data in formats appropriate for computer use and to enter the data into the computer.

Some schools and training facilities may be able to offset these costs by imaginative use of computers when classes are not in session. They may, for example, establish services using the computers, such as desk-top publishing. On the other hand, computer adoption sometimes leads to schools staying open longer, e.g., to provide services to the community, thereby raising expenses without generating additional income.

Management Requirements

The novelty of computers, and hesitation among teachers and other staff regarding this innovation, makes leadership of computer adoption particularly critical. Leadership must start at the national level, with clearly articulated policies and explicit support from the top echelon of the education establishment.

The head of each school or training facility that adopts computers must also support adoption consistently and explicitly. Only such leadership will encourage instructors to invest the time and energy necessary to learn to use computers effectively. Teachers must be convinced that computers will be a permanent and valued part of the educational system.

To bring computers into the education and training system, education policy makers and school staff must address a series of questions for which there are no definitive answers. They must decide:

- what to teach, e.g., programming, regular curriculum;
- how to teach, e.g., CAI, use of personal productivity tools;

- when to teach, e.g., primary, secondary, post-secondary;
- where to teach, e.g., computer lab, regular classroom, vocational classes;
- how to teach teachers;
- whether and how computers can help improve education management, and;
- what is needed to help schools and training facilities use computers effectively.

Whatever the programme design, successful implementation depends on cultural beliefs, teacher training and incentive and support systems.

It is critical that computer adoption be made to fit the daily beliefs of the schools. We distinguish here between "guiding beliefs," i.e., the general long-term values of the educational system, and "daily beliefs," i.e., the actual, day-to-day values that determine behavior in a school. Computers must support the school's daily beliefs, otherwise they will not be used effectively. For example, a guiding belief might be that schools should develop students' abstract, problem-solving ability. In contrast, a daily belief may be that doing well on public multiple-choice exams is most important. If computers are introduced to develop problem-solving abilities at the expense of exam preparation, teachers and students will resist using them.

Teacher training is also critical. Too often, the bulk of budgets for computer adoption goes into hardware, leaving little for training. Yet teacher training will determine how effectively computers are used in schools. Teachers must understand how to use the computers and must develop a sense of "ownership" in the technology—a belief that it can be a valuable and ongoing part of his/her instruction activities. Teachers need sufficient training in the use of the software to feel very comfortable using it. They need training in methods for integrating the computer into their instructional activities and altering instructional activities where appropriate. Training should be designed to fit the specific needs and skills of the educators, the characteristics of the education system and the ways in which the computers will be used. If teachers are expected to use computer-managed instruction, they will need training in the use and interpretation of diagnostic and associated tools.

Administrative and supervisory staff will need training to

understand how best to organize computer use, as well as how to use the computer to improve management. Often this training can be done in the course of ordinary daily use of the computer to maintain records and make management decisions. Clerical staff can generally learn to use the computer on the job.

Clearly, the introduction of computers will raise the workload of teachers and others in the school, at least in the short term. An incentive system that helps motivate all new computer users will therefore be important. Incentives may be tangible, e.g., increases in salary; they may also be intangible, e.g., increased status associated with using this "high technology," or recognition from the central educational authorities. Incentives may also be indirect, e.g., the ability to supplement teaching salaries with part-time work related to computers.

Support systems, particularly peer support among teachers, are also valuable. These systems should enable teachers to resolve hardware and software problems quickly and easily, as well as helping them integrate computers into their instructional activities. Some countries are experimenting with Education Centers that provide support to a number of schools. They evaluate software, help train teachers, provide access to different types of machines, answer questions and help resolve problems with hardware or software.

When possible, a computer co-ordinator at the school should be trained to provide user support, maintain the machines, schedule activities and help plan future adoption and use. It is important to choose co-ordinators carefully, as they must be interested in and committed to helping other teachers gain computer skills. Where the organizational culture discourages sharing information and collegial interaction, the co-ordinator may need special coaching.

Technical Requirements
In addition to the technical requirements that apply to all education technologies, a key requirement for microcomputers is compatibility. If the school wants students to get experience with different types of computer systems, compatibility may not be necessary. In most cases, however, schools will want hardware to be compatible so that different microcomputers can use the same software. This will be particularly important if the school expects

to link the machines on a network. Of course, software must be compatible with (able to run on) the hardware. In addition, peripherals, such as printers, must be compatible with the hardware and software.

Environmental conditions must also support the computer, e.g., there must be a supply of sufficient, reliable power. If there is excessive dust or heat, facilities must protect the machine, or the computer must be one designed to resist those elements.

One of the most important requirements, both for hardware and software, is technical support. Hardware should have service contracts that ensure initially getting the computer up and running, as well as providing ongoing maintenance.

Software should have technical support available to answer questions as users learn to use the software, and to help troubleshoot when problems arise. It is also important to assess the degree of "help" which is built into the software to answer questions about use or help resolve problems.

Opportunities in the Coming Decade

Perhaps most important in the coming decade will be development of clear and meaningful national strategies for effectively using computers in educational and training systems. This is an exercise for the most senior level of the educational establishment.

In order to develop such a strategy, policy makers must first identify the major goals of the education and training system. They can then consider how computers can help achieve those goals. On that basis, a strategy for computer adoption in education can be developed. It is also crucial to recognize, however, that the strategy must be flexible enough to allow individual schools and teachers to adapt computer use to their particular circumstances.

Countries will vary greatly in their national computers-in-education strategies for the coming decade. Some, like Brazil or India, may want the education system to produce computer expertise at many levels of sophistication, in order to compete in global software production markets. If this is the strategic goal, the country may wish to allocate a significant part of its computers-in-education resources to advanced training for a relatively small population of students.

Other countries may want to teach small numbers of people to use computers in particular fields, e.g., CAD/CAM (computer-aided design and manufacturing). Still others may be primarily interested in developing end user skills among students who will use computers for instruction in fields in which the country lacks qualified teachers. The particular set of goals will determine the best approach to computer use in schools and training facilities.

Once the national strategy has been developed, decision-makers will have to identify the requirements for successfully implementing the strategy, and the resources the country has available to fulfill them. In order to do so, they will need access to information about the ways in which computers have been introduced into similar situations, the factors contributing to success and the impact. On the basis of that analysis, an implementation plan can be developed.

If computers in education and training are to be successful in the coming decade, each level of the education and training system must then develop its own computer adoption strategy, in view of the national strategy. It need not be an elaborate plan, but it must identify goals and resources and the requirements for achieving those goals.

It is important to note that by making their strategy explicit, policy makers can better offset undesirable consequences of computer adoption. A good example concerns the issue of inequality. Many developing countries believe that some of the population must be computer literate if the country is to be competitive in world markets in the coming decade. Yet financial constraints make it impossible to give more than a small proportion of students reasonable access to computers while in school.

If a computer education policy is never made explicit, the students receiving computer education are likely to be those already privileged in the society. If the policy is made explicit, however, policy makers can ensure that those receiving computer education include students from groups who would ordinarily be disadvantaged.

A key determinant of the impact of computers in education in developing countries will be software. During the coming decade, educational software will improve and become less expensive. Nonetheless, developing countries will continue to need quality software that is specifically appropriate to their curriculum, culture, circumstances and the skills of teachers and students.

To meet this need, many countries will be able to develop their own courseware using authoring languages. These languages offer the easiest way for non-programmer teachers to develop applications that fit their particular needs and style. Some developing countries, such as India, will have a large skill base in programming that will enable them to develop their own educational software industry. The software they produce can be specifically designed to fit their conditions and needs, and those of other developing countries.

Technological advances will continue to make computers cheaper and more powerful. One of the most important opportunities these changes will offer in the coming decade is for expanding access to information. Developing countries will be able to link local computer centers to national library systems and international data exchange networks, providing access to massive databases. Along with declining costs of satellite-based telecommunications systems, such networks can change the underlying structure of access to information.

Another important technological advance which will become widely available and reasonably priced during the coming decade will be voice recognition systems. This innovation will make computers far easier to use, since the user can simply "talk to" the computer. Along with voice simulation—with which computers can "talk back"—it will enable those with few literacy skills to use computers effectively. If such computers are linked to national and international information networks, they can give people throughout developing countries broad access to information and training. Advances in artificial intelligence will also make computers easier for everyone to use.

To keep apprised of these kinds of developments, and their implications for, and applications in, education and training systems, policy makers will need ways to monitor relevant technological changes. In addition, developing countries will need to undertake and monitor research on computer use in education and training systems like their own. In addition, the coming decade should witness more co-operation among developing countries in exchanging information and experience about computers in education and training in order to develop resources that meet their common needs.

5.7 Interactive Videodisc

Interactive videodisc (IVD) is a powerful technology in which video images and audio information are manipulated by a computer. By convention, videodisc programmes are distinguished by four levels of interactivity:

- Level I: The videodisc shows images in a fixed sequence. The user can only control which frame the player should go to, by number.
- Level II: The videodisc has a limited computer programme which gives the user some additional control.
- Level III: The videodisc player is linked with a computer, providing more complex programme and considerable interactivity. Users can use keyboards, touch screen, and other means to enter information.
- Level IV: A highly complex system that includes two videodisc players and sophisticated computer programming for immediate feedback and interactivity.

References to interactive videodisc in this discussion refer to Level III interactivity. References to videodisc in general refer to all four levels of videodiscs.

Capabilities and Contributions

IVD offers the possibility of real breakthroughs in delivery of instruction via an education technology. The combination of visuals, audio, and interactivity can provide rich simulation experiences that challenge the learner to use knowledge and problem-solving skills in an immediate and interesting way. It is particularly valuable for vocational training because it can offer powerful simulations of "hands-on" experience and because it allows learners to experience different views and conditions for the same process.

For these reasons, despite its relative expense, IVD is being increasingly used in universities, vocational training facilities and businesses in developed countries. Three factors contribute to its rising popularity: consistent, positive reports on its effectiveness; the durability of discs, and; its flexibility in providing instruction to large numbers of widely differing learners.

Although studies of IVD impact are limited in number, those that exist suggest that learners make achievement gains faster and retain material longer using IVD than conventional teaching methods. IVD instruction provides consistent quality, allows easy measurement of competency and knowledge and can be adapted for different audiences.

IVD provides instant access to a vast visual data base, excellent still and motion picture quality, graphics, text and high-quality sound. It can be used by an individual or by groups. Instruction can be tailored according to user capabilities and knowledge. IVD can also allow the learner to control the pace and direction of instruction.

China is the largest developing country user—10,000 players were recently adopted by Ningbo province. IVD is also being used in Saudi Arabia, Indonesia, Ivory Coast, Egypt and Mexico, among other developing countries.

Despite its sophistication and power as a teaching instrument, IVD costs place it beyond the reach of primary and secondary schools even in developed countries. Most, if not all, of IVD use in developed and developing countries is for higher education and technical training.

Nonetheless, as the technology advances and costs drop, it may well become a valuable tool in general education, with uses ranging from data storage to complex interactive instruction. It has also been suggested as an effective tool for training teachers by showing models of effective teaching methods and demonstrating diagnosis of student difficulties in particular subjects (Anzalone:64).

Pedagogical Requirements
A major limitation of IVD for education today is lack of software. Although there is some excellent courseware available, it is often geared to a very specific audience, and may not fit the culture and curriculum of developing countries. In order for IVD to be cost-effective in developing countries, courseware must address the needs of very large numbers of students or fill an important gap in those countries' education and training systems. The versatility and sophistication of IVD makes it very difficult for developing countries to produce or modify the courseware.

Financial Requirements
Microcomputer technology and "authoring" software, which

allows non-programmers to develop software, have greatly reduced costs of IVD during the past 10 years. Nonetheless, it remains a relatively expensive education technology. Within the coming decade, however, technological advances—particularly CD-I, discussed below—will reduce costs tremendously.

Costs of courseware development vary widely depending on several factors, including the level of interactivity, the complexity of the subject matter and instructional design and the type of equipment. In contrast to the rapidly declining costs of delivery systems, development costs will continue to be relatively high.

Management Requirements

The management requirements for IVD are much like those of computers, only more demanding because IVD technology is even more complicated. Although videodisc may seem easier to use than computers, the complexity of the technology will demand considerable changes in teaching and learning styles. As a result, teachers and school administrators will need training in using IVD effectively as a teaching tool and in integrating the technology into ongoing curricula.

New values about teaching are also likely to be necessary. IVD stimulates individual learning, initiative and independent problem solving. In school systems that emphasize rote memorization, new attitudes about education will have to arise. Nor can the process of changing values be done by decree; teachers must be made comfortable with the new technology and the continuing value of their own roles. They must understand why a new style of learning supports the educational goals of their institution and the country. They must understand the critical roles they play in creating change that supports development.

These new values cannot be developed in a vacuum. The incentive system, communication system and other systems in the education establishment must support IVD use and the related changes. Teachers must be rewarded for learning new ways of teaching. Two-way communication between teachers and policy makers will support effective and appropriate use of the new technology.

Technical Requirements

Today, one of the most critical technical requirements of IVD is compatibility between hardware components and between hardware and software. This is a very challenging task. There are still shake-outs going on among manufacturers. There is no commonly accepted standard. Furthermore, it is difficult or impossible to convert software designed to run on one type of system so that it will run on another. Unless the education system has access to expertise that can assist in evaluating and selecting an IVD system, the technical requirements in choosing IVD systems may be beyond most developing country educational systems. As the discussion below notes, most of these technical constraints will be eliminated by CD-I technology.

Opportunities in the Coming Decade

IVD is such a powerful medium that it may well become a valued part of education and training in developing countries in the coming decade. Currently, educators in the developed and developing countries face extremely high cost and technology constraints in any effort to introduce the technology into their institutions.

Technological advances may soon resolve many of those difficulties. CD-ROM (compact disc-read only memory), for example, has been hailed as "one of the most significant technologies for high-density, low-cost information storage" (CD-I News, October 1987, p.4). As costs continue to drop, CD-ROM may play a role as an information and reference resource in developing country education and training systems.

Another technological innovation, CD-I (compact disc-interactive), which is only now coming out in demonstration form, will offer a number of significant breakthroughs:

- tremendous power—combining a powerful microprocessor, stereo quality sound, video pictures, computer animation, and 600 megabytes of programme code and data;
- a universal standard, because all CD-I discs are compatible with all CD-I players;
- ease of use, and;
- relatively low costs—only a color monitor or TV will be necessary to complete the system, and, in the U.S., early costs are about $1,200 to $1,500, with a rapid drop in prices likely to follow.

Because CD-I is so new, the developers of education and

training applications will begin slowly. During the coming decade, however, software is likely to increase dramatically. Because CD-I is standardized, generic programme designers can develop programmes for less investment and have the opportunity for larger markets, without worrying about conversion issues.

This is likely to be an important educational technology by the end of the decade. During the next few years, education policy makers in developing countries can monitor the technology, the development of software, the impact on education and the "success factors" that determine impact. They can also begin to explore ways in which IVD can support more creative learning environments, develop independent problem-solving skills and stimulate individual initiative among learners.

Some developing countries will be interested in using IVD technology before CD-I is available. They may wish to use IVD to meet a large demand for an important area of instruction, where there is a lack of qualified teachers and the interactive, visual and audio features of IVD make it particularly valuable. They may also believe gaining early experience with the technology will serve important national education goals. Pilot projects in these countries can provide valuable information about the "success factors" related to IVD use in their own systems and those of other developing countries.

As is the case with computers, it will be important for education policy makers to begin gaining familiarity with IVD and its capabilities, and to learn how to assess the quality and appropriateness of IVD for the country's needs.

5.8 Hand-held Electronic Devices

Hand-held electronic devices are small, microprocessor-driven machines used to help teach basic spelling and arithmetic skills. Two types appear to have potential value in developing country education systems: electronic learning aids and calculators (Anzalone).

Electronic learning aids generally have voice simulation, a method to enter letters and numbers and drill and practice exercises in arithmetic and language skills. Hand-held calculators are available with many levels of power, from inexpensive calculators that are solar-powered and can perform basic calculations to more expensive devices that can be programmed to perform complex algorithmic operations.

Capabilities and Contributions

Little examination has been made of the use of hand-held electronic devices in developing countries. One study of the use of electronic learning aids in primary school suggests that they can be cost-effective if used over a period of time (Anzalone). They appear to be appropriate for primary education—relatively cheap, easy to use, quite sturdy and battery-operated. The study found that students who used the devices had greater learning gains in language, arts and mathematics than those who did not. Results were about the same among boys and girls. Less able students appeared to benefit more than the other children. Teachers appeared to have positive attitudes about the devices. Students became very involved in using them.

A literature review could not find any published studies of the use of calculators in schools in developing countries (Anzalone). Studies in the U.S., however, suggest that the use of calculators in instruction (but not used on tests) contribute to higher mathematics achievement gains than were produced by instruction without the use of calculators. Studies have found that the use of calculators can help develop students' problem-solving skills, improve computational skills and improve attitudes toward mathematics. It appears that students with less mathematics ability gain more than others by using calculators.

It has been suggested that one benefit of calculators can be to provide those who leave school in the first few years with the means to solve arithmetic problems they will face in work and personal life. Although they may be dependent on the calculator, without it they are unable to solve arithmetic problems at all (Anzalone).

Pedagogical Requirements

The pedagogical requirements for electronic learning aids are minimal. These aids provide very simple drill and practice, and ordinarily the programmes cannot be adapted. If they fit the existing curriculum and approach to teaching arithmetic and language arts, they can usually be integrated fairly easily into class instruction.

In contrast, calculators need to be carefully integrated into the ongoing mathematics instruction. Although this presents a far simpler task than for other education technologies, it will require attention to similar concerns: an approach that fits the curriculum, development of materials that utilize the technology and fit the instruction style of schools and usage patterns that fit the culture and skills of students and teachers.

Financial Requirements

These devices are relatively inexpensive in comparison to many other educational technologies we have discussed. Schools interested in adopting the devices must cover the basic costs: cost of the devices, batteries if not solar-powered and replacements for devices lost or broken.

Management Requirements

Electronic learning devices probably require relatively little management attention. Teachers appear to utilize them easily and without resistance. The devices are easy to fit into ongoing instruction.

One management concern will be distribution and monitoring of the devices. In order to gain economies of scale and make the devices cost-effective, large number of students must use them over a long period of time. To gain large numbers of users, they may be circulated among different grades or schools. Such efforts will complicate distribution and monitoring tasks.

It will be more difficult to manage introduction of calculators. There is considerable suspicion in developing and well as developed countries that calculators create dependency without helping strengthen arithmetic skills. Perhaps the most critical management challenge is convincing instructors and parents that calculators can help develop mathematics skills and can give those who leave school in the early years a means of solving arithmetic problems.

In addition, like other education technologies, calculator adoption must be well managed, with leadership, teachers training, and incentive systems.

Technical Requirements

Once adopted, these devices have few technical requirements, other than ensuring that batteries are available to fit the devices, and that students and teachers understand how to operate them.

Opportunities in the Coming Decade
These devices appear to hold promise as a relatively inexpensive means for improving basic language and arithmetic skills. Although overshadowed by the more sophisticated and dramatic education technologies, they may be able to make significant contributions in the coming decade. What are needed are studies of cost-effectiveness, impact on achievement, value in improving the ability to solve arithmetic problems outside school and success factors associated with using these devices in developing countries.

5.9 Film and Filmstrips
Film offers a wide variety of available materials, many of which are inexpensive or free. It is an effective technology for teaching complex material and motor-perceptual skills. Film can be cost-effective under the following conditions: the film is timely; the material has long-term application; visual effects are important, and; the subject matter is complex and qualified teachers are unavailable.

Yet film is not, in most cases, cost-effective. Equipment is expensive. The content and language of the film must fit the school or training environment, because it cannot be easily adapted. Film does not appear to be superior in delivering instruction in most educational settings, in comparison to conventional teaching or less expensive technologies such as tape-slide presentations. As a general principle, film should be used only when it provides instruction that cannot be delivered in any other way.

In contrast, film loops are more economical than 16mm film. They are easier to use than film, and can be used by individual students. There is also a considerable amount of general education and vocational training material available.

Pedagogical Requirements
The pedagogical requirements for film are much like those of other technologies. Particular care must be taken in obtaining film materials because they can be adapted only with great

difficulty. Short, single-concept films can be more flexible than more elaborate films, and are more easily integrated into curricula. Those interested in identifying films can use directories such as the *Educational Film/Video Locator.*

Financial Requirements
Film is a relatively expensive medium. Projectors are expensive and difficult to maintain. Obtaining film programmes is often expensive for developing countries. Film loops are more likely to fit the budgets of school systems in these countries—both equipment and film materials are much less expensive than those of regular 16mm film.

Management Requirements
Management requirements are similar to those of radio-vision, tape-slide, and video.

Technical Requirements
Like other technologies, film demands skills in equipment operations and maintenance. These skills are often in limited supply in developing countries, particularly in schools.

Opportunities in the Coming Decade
For most developing countries, film is unlikely to be a cost-effective education technology in the coming decade. There are exceptions. India, for example, has an enormous film industry which could develop high-quality educational films designed for its own and other developing country education and training systems. The difficulty is likely to lie in making education films that are appropriate for the variety of cultures and educational approaches within India and in other developing countries, or in making training films that fit specific labor market needs.

CHAPTER SIX

The Role of the United Nations Development Programme

Chapters one to five of this paper focus on the expected education and training related needs of developing countries during the 1990s. Each chapter contains a wide range of recommendations for strategies and programmes that address these needs. Since many Third World nations lack the resources necessary to implement corrective action, our recommendations can also be viewed as a blueprint for international technical co-operation.

All kinds of donors provide assistance to developing countries in the areas of education and training—bilateral programmes, international organizations, private voluntary organizations (PVOs) and private sector institutions. As a co-ordinating and facilitative as well as a funding agency within the UN system, UNDP faces a challenging agenda:

- How to provide meaningful educational support to developing countries without becoming obligated to unattainable levels of aid or impossibly long periods.
- How to achieve better co-ordination among donors whose organizational missions and cultures are so different.
- How to structure co-operation to support broad programme developments as distinct from project support.
- How to support an appropriate level of risk-taking which has the potential for identifying more attractive educational approaches.
- How to develop a pool of international experts committed for an extended period of time and available for short-term technical co-operation upon little advance notice.

Described below are four activities which UNDP should consider undertaking to address this agenda: establishing clear guidelines for the education and training sector projects which it funds (6.1); organizing an international education and training programme consultative council (6.2); providing support for areas of need not being adequately addressed by other donors, e.g. educational technology (6.3), and; promoting responses to the challenge of financial stringency (6.4). The latter involves consideration of how UNDP can help the developing countries and their donors best to defend the claims of the education and training sector for scarce resources against the claims of the other sectors. The question of what UNDP can do to enlighten the millions who will be left entirely out of the main stream of education or training for lack of means to reach them is of equal importance.

6.1 Establish Clear Guidelines for UNDP-funded Education and Training Sector Projects

One of UNDP's major functions is to serve as a funding agency for projects developed by member governments or international organizations such as UNESCO and ILO. If UNDP wants to strengthen its impact in education and training, the agency may wish to adopt a set of guidelines by which the appropriateness of proposals submitted for funding could be judged and project implementation could be evaluated. Guidelines could be universal, i.e., applicable to any proposed project, sectoral specific, e.g., primary, secondary, university level education or geared to the needs of specific geographic regions. Chapters one to five of this paper provide a framework for the development of project guidelines.

The following are examples of possible universal guidelines which could be developed by UNDP:

- How does the proposed project improve educational quality without escalating costs?
- How does the project address the issue of educational equity, i.e., how does it improve access or the equitable distribution of pupils in terms of wealth, gender, rural opportunity?
- What is the proposed project's impact on internal or external educational efficiency?
- To what extent will the recipient country be able to sustain the level of recurrent costs needed to implement the project over the long term?

Secondly, UNDP can develop sector specific guidelines, such as the following:

- To what degree will the project reduce primary school dropout and repeater rates in country x?

- Will unit costs for higher education in country x be reduced as a result of the project?
- What will be the proposed technical/vocational education project's impact on the "informal sector?"
- To what extent will country x's economic infrastructure be able to absorb the graduates of the vocational programme which the proposed project intends to support?

Finally, these are examples of regional specific guidelines:

- For African education projects: to what extent will the proposed project reduce education related unit costs below 983 averages: $48 per primary student; $223 per secondary student; and $2710 per tertiary student? (World Bank, 1988)
- For Asian (and African) projects: to what extent will the proposed project provide increased access for female students?

6.2 Organize an International Education and Training Programme Consultative Council

UNDP serves as a co-ordinating body for programmes administered by the specialized agencies of the UN system in developing countries. It would be consistent with UNDP's principal role, therefore, if it were to initiate the formation of an international consultative council for education and training programmes. UNDP could serve as the convenor or co-ordinating agency for this International Consultative Council on Education and Training.

In other technical areas, e.g., nutrition and health, UN-supported consultative bodies play an important role in focusing donor agency priorities and in disseminating state-of-the-art information. Yet to our knowledge, no such body exists in the education and training area. There is, however, an enormous need. Charter membership in such a council should include the major UN agencies with education and training related activities, i.e., UNDP, UNESCO, ILO, and the World Bank; and major bilateral agencies, e.g., USAID, NORAD, DANIDA, GTZ, etc. Consideration also ought to be given to participation on the part of relevant PVOs, private sector organizations and distinguished technical experts. The following are some of the important functions which could be served by the proposed Council.

The development of consensus on priority needs, strategies and programmes

The situation now with regard to education and training is somewhat chaotic. Each major donor agency seems to be pursuing its own programming with little attempt at co-ordination. There are certain advantages to such a "free market" approach, i.e., institutional initiative and innovation are encouraged. On the other hand, lack of co-ordination facilitates a "re-invention of the wheel" syndrome, and makes it difficult for recipient countries to make the best of international technical assistance. For example, more could be done to co-ordinate the efforts of those working in education with those working in training. The proposed Council would sponsor a dialogue among participating agencies regarding strategies for addressing major problems of UNDP member countries. Such a dialogue should facilitate the building of consensus around what needs to be done, and the role that each participating agency can play in addressing targeted needs.

An Education and Training Information Clearinghouse

There currently is no central locus of information for those interested in "what is going on" or "who is doing what" in the important fields of education and training. The absence of a project/programme clearinghouse makes the task of trying to co-ordinate activities even more difficult. Were UNDP to strengthen its co-ordinator's role in education and training, the organization and operation of such an information exchange would seem to be a natural undertaking. Perhaps such a clearinghouse could be organized in the form of an electronic data base, which could be easily updated, and to which users could subscribe. The data base's foundation could be built by accessing information on the programmes and projects of the participating institutions of the proposed international co-ordinating council.

Review State-of-the-Art Issues and Technical Approaches

The proposed Council could also serve as a review panel for important issues and new strategies/methods/technologies for addressing the education and training related problems of developing countries. Specific meetings could be convened to hear presentations made by educational planners and other technical experts who have developed new approaches to solving problems that could make a difference. Review by the Council would help give sanction to the new methodology and facilitate its dissemination and use in the Third World.

6.3 Provide Support for Areas of Need Not Being Adequately Addressed by Other Donors

UNDP has an important role to play in terms of providing support for education and training related areas of need not being adequately addressed by other donors. Support should be provided in a targeted manner so that as a result of UNDP assistance lessons are learned about the viability of particular approaches or techniques. Areas of assistance should be carefully selected in order to maximize the impact of UNDP support and avoid stretching the agency too thin. One area that deserves immediate attention is the field of education technology.

The application of education technology in the Third World at present is receiving relatively little in the way of funding support despite its demonstrated potential for addressing education and training needs (see Chapters four and five). UNDP is in the position of being able to play an important role in enhancing the application of such relevant technologies as print, radio, micocomputers, audio and/or teleconferencing.

In this connection, it may be noted that, from 1977 to 1986, UNDP allocated $590,210,048 to education projects in developing countries; and, from 1968 to 1988, $699,244,580 on vocational training projects. Only $4,807,293 was used to fund educational technology projects (as defined in Chapter four) during this period, which represents only 0.8 per cent of total expenditures on education and training projects.

Other donors have been equally negligent in this area. The World Bank has provided support to a number of textbook production projects, and an innovative television education project in China. USAID has been instrumental in developing and successfully testing primary school interactive radio-based curricula. However, aside from these and several other "notable exceptions," there has been little in the way of significant support. Much effort to date has gone into the establishment of a basic educational infrastructure, i.e., building schools and establishing educational planning and training institutions.

Given the role that education technology can play in addressing two of the most important education and training issues in the 1990s, i.e., "quality" and "access," it would seem imperative that international donors begin to play a more supportive role. An opportunity exists for UNDP to provide institutional leadership to its member countries as well as to other international donors. The following are some steps that could be taken.

Give Funding Priority to Projects that Utilize Education Technology
Guidelines could be developed to help UNDP field offices and member country government agencies develop appropriate proposals for funding. Perhaps a certain percentage of available funds could be earmarked for education technology projects. These projects should focus on such areas as developing national education technology strategies; strengthening the education and training policy, planning and administrative infrastructure; developing programmes to integrate education technology into existing instructional training programmes; building up the capacity of developing countries to create high quality courseware, and; developing prototypes of successful education technology programmes.

Form a UNDP Education Technology Advisory Committee
UNDP at present lacks extensive in-house education technology expertise. The agency is not structured to provide extensive technical backstopping to member countries. To guide its work in education technology, we recommend the creation of an advisory committee of six to eight experts, who could assist UNDP in developing project guidelines, reviewing proposals and evaluating projects. Membership on the Committee should include both technology (hardware) specialists, experts in instructional design and pedagogy and those with experience in the application of technologies to Third World conditions.

Fund Pilot Projects in New and Promising Technologies
Some education technologies hold great promise. Some have already proved their value in the industrialized world but still need to be tested in a developing country setting. Interactive

videodisc is one example. Pilot projects will be necessary in order to assess the effectiveness of such technologies, and to determine the programme design features that will make them most effective in the Third World. UNDP can help to conduct and evaluate such pilot projects, and disseminate findings to developing countries and other donor agencies.

Fund Projects which Provide Support to Expand the Use of Proven Educational Technologies
Certain aspects of educational technology already have demonstrated particular effectiveness in improving education and/or training quality and delivery. Examples include the use of interactive radio-based instruction to teach primary school mathematics, science, and language arts; the use of teleconferencing to deliver in-service training to teachers as well as to relieve shortages in specialized technical, managerial, and scientific talent, and; the use of hand-held calculators as an aid in the learning of basic mathematics. UNDP should look for opportunities to strengthen the work of countries which already have successfully invested in education technology and seek to build upon what already has been accomplished.

6.4 Promote Responses to the Challenge of Financial Stringency

The servicing of crushing foreign debt, the implementation of austerity and restructuring policies and the reduction of domestic and external financial deficits will continue to impose limitations and in some cases reductions of expenditures on education and training in many developing countries. Scarce foreign exchange will be severely rationed under priorities established for this and other sectors. We have indicated that UNDP may promote and support fully realistic responses to these difficulties by focusing on how to make the most productive, effective and relevant use of the limited resources available for education and training.

Beyond that, however, other responses to the financial realities will be expected of UNDP. One question, for example, is how can UNDP help the developing countries and their donors best to defend the claims of the education and training sector for scarce resources against the claims of the other sectors? Secondly, what can UNDP do to enlighten the millions who will be left entirely out of the mainstream of education or training for lack of means to reach them?

Education versus the financial crunch
The first of these responses is a part of UNDP's role to give leadership, together with bodies like the World Bank and the Organisation for Economic Cooperation and Development, in the promotion of sound economic planning and policy in the Third World. UNDP would be well-advised to support a systematic enquiry, perhaps jointly with the other bodies mentioned, into how education and training can and do help a nation to combat the financial crunch. Some substantive issues to be addressed in this enquiry may be evoked by the following thoughts.

Nearly all the values, even the cultural, political and spiritual, derived from sound education have a positive financial aspect. Cheap sources of contentment not subject to depletion can displace some of the demand for costly material satisfactions. Boredom and consumerism are bedfellows. Citizenship and understanding of the national need for austerity and equitable burden-sharing reduce the risk of destructive disturbances and counter-productive tendencies. This beneficial impact of education generally may be reinforced by education in citizenship specifically.

To the extent that "people get the government they deserve," a well-educated electorate, and education of the elected, assists the selection of national leaders qualified and motivated to give the nation sound economic and financial management. Even in the poorest countries, some money still squandered and diverted could in future be saved for education and other needs.

Resources other than money should also be saved, as shown in the following instances. Women are generally exploited, but yet are rarely enabled to realise their full potential in economic roles. Better education paves the way for their access to the life of the nation. Other sections of the masses who have very low income may find remunerative opportunities when trained.

The military sector may not be fully cost-effective in delivering security, nor use idle time and resources for useful non-military purposes, including education and training of the defence personnel. Wherever the soldiers make or break governments, they are liable to intervene harmfully if poorly educated, whereas public-spirited and enlightened soldiers have provided better government than have other non-elected politicians.

Population and health are two major areas where education

has economic as well as general significance. A great aggravating factor in the poverty of less endowed countries is over-population and excessive population growth. In most African countries, including some still making impressive gains in production, the rate of population growth exceeds the rate of increase in gross national product. Little further study may be necessary to confirm unquestionably that education of women is the most potent of the factors contributing to reductions in the birth rate.

There is a strong body of opinion among doctors with extensive international experience that the biggest single contributor to improvements in health is more and better education—not medical treatment. This fits in with the fact that the human body has considerable powers of self-recuperation, especially when it is left free of abuse and ignorant interference. This fact has great financial significance in view of the cost of medical treatment and above all in view of the cost of sickness and disablement in terms of lost production and diminished human performance.

Also having these adverse economic and financial effects, and assimilable to sickness, are addiction to alcohol, tobacco, drugs, and violence, cruelty and sexual abnormalities associated with flawed upbringing and mental and emotional disorders. Even such problems can be mitigated by education. They are customarily combatted by police action and imprisonment, and curative (more than preventive) medicine, all of which can be more costly than education and simply contain the problem rather than solving it.

Then, in more direct and measurable ways, education and training provide significant economic and financial returns. The increase in people's income following their instruction can occur much more quickly in the case of training than in that of education, a longer-term process than training. However, also to be credited to the education sector are the gains in earnings from training made fully effective only when preceded by adequate education.

In the final calculation, earnings attributable to education are those made possible by higher productivity derived from education and not to earnings related to factors other than personal performance and output.

The relevance of education and training to the requirements

of employers makes education a productive and fruitful investment. Repeatedly in this report, and in the responses to the survey (see Annex I), the point is made that the education system must be designed to render the human output employable and more productive, with due but not overriding regard for other values of education.

Some education and training systems in developing countries, and related foreign aid received, may still be excessively focused on curricular and educational objectives set by, and for needs of, developed countries with widely different cultures and economic conditions. The net loss in financial return from education due to this factor may be lower than the non-financial loss, at least in the short-run.

Education should duly contribute to building a bridge, and narrowing the difference, between the developing and developed countries. It should equip citizens for employment abroad as well as at home, especially citizens of developing countries with grave over-population, unemployment and under-employment. The investment in educating and training people who emigrate—the "brain drain"—is incorrectly regarded as a total loss for the country that "exports" them. Some will return home with their valuable added knowledge and experience. Most will gain financially abroad more than they could by staying home, and they will share this gain with the relatives and friends they left behind. Remittances from emigrants are a major source of national and foreign exchange income for a growing number of developing countries.

In any event, it is vital for developing countries facing enormous financial difficulties to ensure that their education and training dollar brings the largest, quickest return by raising people's employability and productivity in full concordance with the requirements and economic potentialities of their own economy.

It is recommended that UNDP explore these and related issues more deeply and publicize the findings. In association with this exercise in analysis, it would be well in parallel to conduct evaluations of the experience of countries that have made very large investments in the expansion of their education system to identify the extent to which, and the way in which, this has led to satisfactory financial and economic returns. In the data available on UNDP and World Bank aid to education, country by country, it is noticeable that some countries have received very substantially more assistance than others and have chosen to give education conspicuously high priority.

The available data are less complete and conclusive regarding trends in the level and proportions of foreign aid to education and training (see Annex II in this report). It is known that the proportion of UNDP aid going in this direction has been diminishing for a long time up to the present. It is necessary for UNDP to examine now whether this decline should continue or whether it would be justifiable to arrest and reverse it. Relevant considerations for UNDP in this regard may also be of interest for particular countries when they consider the proportion of national resources going to the education sector. UNDP could give guidance and assistance by sharing with them its deliberations and conclusions on this point and by taking account of their views.

Reaching the excluded millions
The second of two responses to the situation imposed by financial stringency concerns what UNDP can do to meet the need for knowledge and skills of the millions who will be left entirely out of the mainstream of education or training for lack of means to reach them. A combination of economy cuts, of emphasis on quality more than quantity in the supply of education and training, and continued population outpacing economic growth, will by the new century leave more people than ever—up to half of the world's larger population—in ignorance, isolation and inability to work productively. Considerations of human solidarity, politics, economics and social stability require that a start be made without delay, at a manageable cost, to bring enlightenment to a growing proportion of these marginal lives.

Where even pencils, paper and textbooks for school children are difficult to pay for, the instruments of modern technology discussed in Chapter five all seem way beyond reach. But this is not true of radio. A radio transmitter reaching millions of listeners through hundreds of radios in public places involves equipment costing less per listener than the cost of one pencil. The programmes transmitted are a significant continuing cost, especially if raised above the normal quality-level of broadcasts received in poor countries, if adapted to combine entertainment with education in an attractive form and if prepared exclusively for the population of a small country.

Broadcasts from larger and more developed countries, though of some value to many, do not really solve this problem. Long-distance receivers cost slightly more per head. More serious is the language barrier, since the widely known international languages like English, French, Spanish, Arabic, etc., are not known to the uneducated people and to those of indigenous groups little touched by colonisation. Russian and Chinese and other languages of major broadcasting countries are known only to elite people from poor countries who have studied abroad in those tongues. However, both radio and TV programmes can be dubbed in any languages required for foreign consumption.

Most serious is the fact that the excellent educational radio programmes broadcast by advanced countries with universal education systems are not at all adapted to the needs, circumstances and culture of people with no education at all. Furthermore, research has sadly demonstrated that the best educational broadcasts anywhere which are disseminated passively rather than interactively to anyone who happens to be listening do not make a worthwhile and lasting educational impact on either children or adults. More positively, it has been found that educational broadcasts addressed to out-of-school listeners can make a real educational impact if conducted interactively within a properly conceived pedagogical framework tailored to the requirements of the audience.

Hence, international co-operation is needed to enlighten the world's vast marginal populations by radio along the following lines:

- financial and technical support of the advanced countries, including use of their radio programming facilities, in the preparation and recording of educational programmes suited to the target populations;
- programmes designed and delivered to well-identified and analysed audiences within an effective pedagogical framework and delivery system embodying well-proven experience with interactive radio techniques;
- programmes prepared on a continuing basis may be periodically updated, expanded and differentiated to be adapted to world

regional and cultural differences while at the same time incorporating a core of basic and accurate knowledge and the most modern and well-tried skills and technologies which are useful everywhere;
* programmes available progressively in more and more languages, starting with the most widely understood languages, and;
* programmes then made available to the broadcasting stations of the developing countries for them to air as they choose.

There should be widespread collaboration between the radio producers and broadcasting studios of the different countries supporting this project, so as to maximise the sources of knowledge, experience and pedagogical capacity drawn upon, and to minimise the cost to each donor by spreading the burden of programming and translation.

In parallel, UNDP could provide technical assistance to countries concerning the production of cheap but effective radio receivers more widely accessible to adults and children in public places, even in the most remote communities. It could also help countries which need to upgrade the power and territorial coverage of their radio broadcasting facilities so as to increase the impact of this project.

UNDP appears to be the best, and perhaps the only really appropriate, co-ordinator of a project of this kind. UNDP is officially a politically and culturally neutral institution. As such, it should be able to establish and win wide support for guidelines designed to protect the listening audiences from propaganda or from political or cultural biases in the programmes presented. Under its surveillance, the project implementers will adhere to the principles, values and recommendations embodied in the constitutions and other instruments, declarations, agreements and conventions and resolutions of the International Organizations and Programmes making up the United Nations family.

It may appear difficult to attain this ideal of neutrality and objectivity, and to win widespread confidence in the UN system's capacity to guarantee it. However, it may be recalled that two or three national or religious radio programmes addressed to a worldwide audience have gained faithful listeners in many countries with widely different beliefs and viewpoints and have earned reputations for their close approaches to verity and objectivity on occasion.

It might take no more than one per cent of UNDP's resources, applied consistently over a decade or more, to make this a viable and lasting activity to educate and train the world's millions who will never go to school and may never even have an employer to give them the least on-the-job training.

List of References

Chapter One: Education

AASCU. 1978. *Futures Creating Paradigm: A Guide to Long-Range Planning.* Washington, D.C.: American Association of State Colleges and Universities.

Alioto, Robert F. and Junghwee. 1975. *J.A. Operational PPBS for Education.* New York: Harper and Row.

Allan, Donald. 1988. A Grand Alliance. *Development Forum 16* (Mar/Apr).

Anzalone, Stephen. 1986. *Using Instructional Hardware for Primary Education in Developing Countries.* Project Bridges.

Armstrong, Gregory. 1984. Implementing Educational Policy: Decentralization of Nonformal Education in Thailand. *Comparative Education Review* 28 (Aug).

Ayres, Robert U. 1969. *Technological Forecasting and Long-range Planning.* New York: McGraw-Hill.

Benson, Charles. 1978. The Economics of Public Education. Boston, MA: Houghton Mifflin.

Brown, Hubert. 1986. Primary Schooling and the Rural Responsibility System in the People's Republic of China. *Comparative Education Review* 30 (Aug).

Cunningham, William. 1982. *Systematic Planning for Educational Change.* Palo Alto, CA: Mayfield Publishing Company.

Danskin, Edith. 1983. Increasing Opportunities for Higher Education: Implications of the Thai Solution. *EDC Occasional Papers.* London: University of London Institute of Education.

Davis, Russell G. 1966. *Planning Human Resource Development.* Chicago: Rand McNally.

—.1980. *Planning Education for Development Vol I: Issues and Problems in the Planning of Education in Developing Countries, Vol II: Models and Methods for Systematic Planning of Education.* Cambridge, MA: Center for Studies in Education and Development, Harvard University.

Dove. 1986. *Teachers and Teacher Education in Developing Countries,* London: Croom Helm.

Ekeh, Helen and Joshua Adeniyi. 1985/86. Using Teachers as Change Agents in the Control of Tropical Diseases — An Extracurricular Approach. *International Quarterly of Community Health Edcuation* 6, No. 4.

Fuller, Bruce. 1986. Is Primary School Quality Eroding in the Third World? *Comparative Education Review* 30 (Nov).

—, K. Gorman, and J. Edwards. 1986. *The Quality of Education and Economic Development.* Washington, D.C.: World Bank.

Ginsburg, Mark and Beatrice Arias-Gondinez. 1984. Nonformal Education and Social Reproduction/Transformation: Educational Radio in Mexico. *Comparative Education Review* 28 (Feb).

Hallak, Jacques. 1976. *La Mise en Place de Politiques Educatives: Role et Methodologie de la Carte Scolaire.* Paris: UNESCO.

Hartley, Harry J. 1968. *Educational Planning-Programming-Budgeting: A Systems Approach.* Englewood Cliffs, NJ: Prentice-Hall.

Heyneman & Jamison. 1984. Textbooks in the Philippines: Evaluation of the Pedagogical Impact of a Nationwide Investment. *Educational Evaluation and Policy Analysis* 6, No. 2 (Summer).

Heyneman & Loxley. 1983. The Effect of Primary School Quality on Academic Achievement across 29 High and Low Income Countries. *American Journal of Sociology* 88, No. 6 (May).

Hopkins, David and William F. Massy. 1981. *Planning Models for Colleges and Universities.* Stanford, CA: Stanford University Press.

Horn, Robin and Ana-Maria Abrigada. 1986. *The Educational Attainment of the World's Population: Three Decades of Progress.* World Bank Discussion Paper.

Hussain, Khateeb M. 1973. *Development of Information Systems for Education.* Englewood Cliffs, NJ: Prentice-Hall.

Johnstone, J. 1980. *Indicators of Education Systems.* Paris: IIEP.

Montero-Sieburth. 1987. *Classroom Management: Instructional Strategies and the Allocation of Learning Resources.* Project Bridges.

Organisation for Economic Cooperation and Development. 1983. *Educational Planning: A Re-Appraisal.* Paris: OECD.

Parnes, Herbert S. 1963. *Planning Education for Economic and Social Development.* Paris: OECD, The Mediterranean Region Project.

Schiefelbein, Ernesto and Russell Davis. 1974. *Development of Educational Planning Models and Application in the Chilean School Reform.* Lexington Books (D.C. Heath and Co).

Thiagarajan & Pasigna. 1986. *Literature Review on the Soft*

Technologies of Learning. Institute for International Research, Project Bridges.
Tilak, Jandahyala. 1987. *Education and Unemployment in India,* New Delhi: Institute of Educational Planning.
UNESCO. 1987. *Statistical Yearbook.*
World Bank. 1986. *Financing Education in Developing Countries.* Washington, D.C.: IBRD.
World Bank. 1986. *Distance Education: An Economic and Educational Assessment of its Potential for Africa.* IBRD.
World Bank. 1988. *Education in Sub-Saharan Africa, A World Bank Policy Study.* IBRD. World Bank Staff Reports.

Chapter Two: Training

Alfthan, T. 1985. Developing Skills for Technological Change: Some Policy Issues. *International Labour Review* 124 (5): 817-29.
Altbach, P.G. 1983. Key Issues of Textbook Provision in the Third World. *Prospects* 13 (3): 315-325.
Anderson, D. 1982. *Small Industry in Developing Countries.* Washington, D.C.: World Bank.
Anderson, L.W. 1987. The Classroom Environment Study: Teaching for Learning. *Comparative Education Review* 31 (2): 69-87.
Behrman, J.R. and N. Birdsall. 1983. The Quality of Schooling: Quantity Alone is Misleading. *The American Economic Review* 73 (5): 928-46.
Blank, W.E. 1982. *Handbook for Developing Competency-Based Training Programs.* Englewood Cliffs, N.J.: Prentice-Hall.
Blaug, M. 1984. *Education and the Employment Problem in Developing Countries.* Geneva: International Labour Organisation.
Block, J. Mastery Learning: The Current State of the Craft. *Educational Leadership* 37:114-117.
—, and R. Burns. 1976. *Review of Educational Research in Education* 4:114-117.
Bloom, B.S. 1976. *Human Characteristics and School Learning.* New York: McGraw-Hill.
Bourke, S. 1985. The Study of Classroom Contexts and Practice. *Teaching and Teacher Education* 1 (1): 33-50.
Bowles, D.W. 1988. *A.I.D.'s Experience with Selected Employment Generation Projects.* Washington, D.C.: U.S. A.I.D.

Bray, M. 1985. High School Selection in Less Developed Countries and the Quest for Equity: Conflicting Objectives and Opposing Pressures. *Comparative Education Review* 20 (2): 216-227.

Braun, F. 1987. Vocational Training as a Link Between the Schools and the Labour Market: The Dual System in the Federal Republic of Germany. *Comparative Education* 23 (2): 123-143.

Brookover, W., C. Beady, P. Flood, J. Schweitzer and J. Wisenbaker. 1979. *School Social Systems and Student Achievement: Schools Can Make a Difference.* New York: Praeger Publishers.

Brophy, J. and T.L. Good. 1986. Teacher Behavior and Student Achievement, in: M.C. Whittrock, *Handbook of Research on Teaching* 3rd ed. New York: Macmillan Publishing Co.

Brown, B.A. 1981. *Characteristics of Industry-Based and Labor-Based Training and Educational Programs, Including Uses of Information Technology in Such Programs: An Overview.* Washington, D.C.: U.S. Office of Technology Assessment.

Castro, C.M. 1979. Vocational Education and the Training of Industrial Labour in Brazil. *International Labour Review,* 118(50): 617-629.

Centra, J.A. and D.A. Potter. 1980. School and Teacher Effects: An Interrelation Model. *Review of Educational Research* 50(2): 273-291.

Chapman, D.W. and D.M. Windham. 1985. Academic Program "Failures" and the Vocational School "Fallacy": Policy Issues in Secondary Education in Somalia. *International Educational Development* 5 (4): 269-281.

Cohen, E. and R.A. Rossmiller. 1987. Research on Effective Schools: Implications for Less Developed Countries. *Comparative Education Review* 31(3): 377-399.

Colclough, C. 1982. The impact of primary schooling on economic development: A review of the evidence. *World Development* 10 (93): 167-185.

Corcoran, T.B. and B.L. Wilson. 1986. *The Search for Successful Secondary Schools: The First Years of the Secondary School Recognition Program.* Washington, D.C.: Office of Educational Research and Improvement, U.S. Department of Education.

Corvalan, O.V. 1979. *Vocational Training in Latin America: A*

Comparative Perspective. Monographs on Comparative and Area Studies in Adult Education. Vancouver, British Columbia: Center for Continuing Education, The University of British Columbia.

—. 1983. Vocational Training and Disadvantaged Youth in Developing Countries. *International Labour Review* 122 (3): 367-381.

Cuervo, A.G. 1985. *Employer-Based Training Survey: Panama.* Washington, D.C.: Bureau for Science and Technology, United States Agency for International Development.

Denham, C. and A. Lieberman. 1980. *Time to Learn.* Washington, D.C.: National Institute of Education.

Dougherty, C. 1989. Cost-Effectiveness of National Training Systems in Developing Countries: Issues and Experience. Washington, D.C.: Education and Employment Division, Population and Human Resources Department, World Bank.

Doyle, W. 1986. Classroom Organization and Management, in: M.C. Whittrock, ed., *Handbook of Research on Teaching.* New York: Macmillan Co.

Ducci, M.A. 1980. The Vocational Training Process in the Study of Latin America: An Interpretative Study. *Studies and Monographs* 47. Montevideo, Centerfore.

—. 1983. Vocational Training: An Open Way. *Studies and Monographs* 62. Montevideo: Centerfore.

Frazer, B.J., H.J. Walberg, W.W. Welch, and J.A. Hattie. 1987. Synthesis of Educational Productivity Research. *International Journal of Educational Research* 11 (2): 145-252.

Fuller, B. 1985. *Raising School Quality in Developing Countries: What Investments Boost Learning?* Washington, D.C.: Education and Training Department, World Bank.

Hanushek, E.A. 1981. Throwing Money at Schools. *Journal of Policy Analysis and Management* 1 (1): 19-41.

Herschbach, D.R. 1984. *Addressing Vocation Training and Retraining Through Educational Technology: Policy Alternatives.* Columbus, Ohio: The National Center for Research in Vocational Education.

—. 1984. *Vocational Planning for Developing Countries: Curricular and Educational Technology Alternatives.* Washington, D.C.: Bureau for Science and Technology, U.S. Agency for International Development.

—. 1985. *Linking Training and Employment: An Emerging Perspective.* Washington, D.C.: Bureau for Science and Technology, U.S. Agency for International Development.

—. 1988. *Improving Training Quality in Developing Countries: Toward Greater Instructional Efficiency.* Washington, D.C.: Education and Employment Division, World Bank.

—, B.A. Rheinhart, R.L. Darcy and J.A. Sanguinetty. 1985. *Linking Training and Employment: A Case Study of Training Systems in Jordan.* Washington, D.C.: Bureau for Science and Technology, U.S. Agency for International Development.

Hershfield, A.E. 1982. Developing Technology to Enhance the Educational Progress, in: *Technology and Educational Policy Implementation Evaluation.* Washington, D.C.: The Institute for Educational Leadership.

Heyneman, S.P., J.P. Farrell and M.A. Sepulveda-Stuardo. 1981. Textbooks and Achievement in Developing Countries: What We Know. *Journal of Curriculum Studies* 13 (4): 277-246.

International Labour Organisation. 1987. *The Role of the ILO in Technical Co-operation.* Report VI, International Labour Conference, 73rd Session. Geneva: International Labour Organisation.

—. 1987. *Training and Retraining—Implications of Technological Change.* Fourth European Regional Conference, Report III. Geneva: International Labour Office.

Kaneko, M. 1984. Education and labor force composition in Southeast and East Asian development. *Developing Economies* 22(1): 47-68.

Kelly, T., D. Evans, V. Faulds and J. Callejas. 1985. *Addressing Employment Needs: A Study of the Training System in Honduras.* Washington, D.C.: Bureau of Science for Technology, U.S. Agency for International Development.

Knapper, C.K. 1982. *Evaluating Instructional Technology.* New York: John Wiley and Sons.

Kyle, R.M.J. 1985. *Reaching for Excellence.* Washington, D.C.: U.S. Government Printing Office.

Leithwood, K.A. and D.J. Montgomery. 1982. The Role of the Elementary School Principal in Program Improvement. *Review of Educational Research* 52 (8): 309-339.

Lipson, J.I. 1981. Changing Organizational Structures to Capitalize on Technology, in: *Technology and Educational Policy*

Implementation Evaluation. Washington, D.C.: The Institute for Educational Leadership.

Lockheed, M.E., S.C. Vail and Fuller. How Textbooks Affect Achievement in Developing Countries: Evidence from Thailand. *Education Evaluation and Policy Analysis* 8 (4): 379-392.

Lysakowski, R.S. and H.J. Walberg. 1982. Instructional Effects of Cues, Participation, and Corrective Feedback: A Quantitative Synthesis. *American Educational Research Journal* 19(4): 559-578.

Maley, D. 1975. *Cluster Concept in Vocational Education.* Chicago: American Technical Society.

Marsden, K. 1984. Services for Small Firms: The Roles of Government Programmes and Market Networks in Thailand. *International Labour Review* 123 (2): 211-235.

McLaughlin, S.D. 1981. *The Wayward Mechanic: An Analysis of Skill Acquisition in Ghana.* Amherst, Massachusetts: Center for International Education.

Metcalf, D.H. *The Economics of Vocational Training: Past Evidence and Future Considerations.* Washington, D.C.: World Bank Staff Working Papers, World Bank.

Middleton, J. and T. Demsky. 1988. *Review of World Bank Investments in Vocational Education and Training for Industry.* Washington, D.C.: Education and Employment Division, Population and Human Resources Department, World Bank.

Noah, H. and J. Middleton. 1987. *Planning and Labor Market Linkages in Chinese Secondary Vocational and Technical Education.* Washington, D.C.: Education and Employment Division, Population and Human Resources Department, World Bank.

Office of Technology Assessment. 1982. *Information Technology and Its Impact on American Education.* Washington, D.C.: U.S. Office of Technology Assessment.

Papola, T.S. 1981. *Urban Informal Sector in a Developing Economy.* New Delhi: Vilcas Publishing House.

Peterson, P.L. and H.J. Walberg (eds.). 1979. *In Search of Excellence: Lessons from America's Best Run Companies.* Berkeley: McCutchan.

Psacharopoulos, G. To Vocationalize or Not to Vocationalize? That Is the Curriculum Question. *International Review of Education* 33(2): 187-211.

Psacharopoulos, G. and M. Woodhall. 1985. *Education and*

Development: Analysis of Investment Choices. New York: Oxford University Press.

Purkey, S.C. and M.S. Smith. 1983. Effective Schools: A Review. *The Elementary School Journal* 83(4): 427-452.

Rosenholtz, S.J. 1985. Effective Schools: Interpreting the Evidence. *American Journal of Education* 93:353-389.

Rosenshine, B.V. 1979. Content, Time and Direct Instruction, in: P.L. Peterson and H.L. Walberg (eds.). *Research on Teaching: Concepts, Findings and Implications.* Berkeley: McCutchan.

Rowan, B., S.T. Bossert and D.C. Dwyer. 1983. Research of Effective Schools: A Cautionary Note. *Educational Researcher,* 12 (4): 24-31.

Salome, B. and J. Charmes. 1988. *In-Service Training: Five Asian Experiences.* Paris: Development Centre of the Organisation for Economic Co-operation and Development.

Schill, W.J. and J.P. Arnold. 1965. *Curricula Content for Six Technologies.* Urbana, Illinois: Bureau of Educational Resources, University of Illinois.

Squires, D.A., W.G. Huitt and J.K. Segars. 1985. *Effective Schools and Classrooms: A Research-Based Perspective.* Alexandria, Virginia: Association for Supervision and Curriculum Development.

Staley, E. 1971. *Planning Occupational Education and Training for Development.* New York: Praeger Publishers.

United States Agency for International Development. 1984. *Botswana Education and Human Resource Sector Assessment.* Washington, D.C.: Bureau of Science and Technology, United States Agency for International Development.

Van Steenwyk, N. 1984. *Vocational Instruction in Honduras: Industrial, Artisan and Computer Training.* Tegucigalpa: U.S. Agency for International Development.

Wagner, L. 1982. *The Economics of Educational Media.* New York: St. Martin's Press.

Wang, M.C. and C.M. Lindvall. 1984. Individual Differences and School Learning Environments, in: Edmund W. Gordon (ed.). *Review of Research in Education.* Washington, D.C.: American Educational Research Association.

Watanabe, S. 1986. Labour-Saving Versus Work-Amplifying Effects of Micro-Electronics. *International Labour Review,* 125 (3): 242-259.

Westphal, L.E., W.R. Yung and G. Pursell. 1981. *Korean Industrial Competence: Where It Comes From.* Washington, D.C.: World Bank.

White, P.B. 1982. Educational Technology Research: Towards the Development of a New Agenda. *British Journal of Educational Technology* 11 (3): 170-177.

World Bank. 1986. *Regional Reviews of Alternative Modes of Vocational Training and Technical Education.* Final Report. Washington, D.C.: Education and Manpower Development Division, Europe, Middle East and North Africa, World Bank.

—. 1987. *World Development Report 1987.* New York: Oxford University Press.

Zucker, A. Computers in Education: National Policy in the USA. *European Journal of Education* 17(4): 395-410.

Zymelman, M. *The Economic Evaluation of Vocational Training Programs.* Baltimore: The Johns Hopkins University Press.

Chapter Three: Manpower Planning

Davis, Russell G. 1988. Planning Techniques and Methods. *International Encyclopedia of Education and Research I,* Supplementary (Nov). Oxford: Pergamon Press.

—. 1988. Manpower Planning Methods. in Russell G. Davis, *Planning Education for Development* II. *Models and Methods for Systematic Planning of Education.* Cambridge: Harvard CSED. pp. 163-278.

FAO. 1984. *Trained Agricultural Manpower Assessment in Africa.* Rome: FAO.

—. 1985. *Institutional Development and Training Programs in Africa.* Rome.

Hudson Institute. 1987. *Workforce 2000.* Indianapolis.

Swanson, B. and W. Reeves. 1986. *Agricultural Research Eastern and Southern Africa: Manpower and Training.* Washington, D.C.: IBRD.

Small Industry and Entrepreneurial Development

Harper, Malcolm. 1984. *Small Business in the Third World.* Englewood Cliffs, NJ: John Wiley.

Selby, A.K. 1981. *Entrepreneurship in Development.* Crompton Press.

EDP Development

Patel, V.G. 1985. *Entrepreneurship Development Programmes in India*. Ahmedabad: Entrepreneurship Development Institute of India.

Government Support Policies and Programmes

Dominguez, Jose. 1986. *Training for Productive Employment: The Case of Spain* (mimeo World Bank conference paper).
Quevedo, Jose. 1985. *Technical Entrepreneurship and Technological Progress in Developing Countries*. Brazil: UNFSSTD.

General Economic

Steel, W. and Y. Takagi. 1983. Small Enterprise Development and the Employment-Output Trade-Off. World Bank Reprint 305.
Davis, Russell G. 1980. Issues and Problems in the Planning of Education in Developing Countries (Chapter 11, "A Case Study of Self-Employment Training"). *Planning Education for Development* I. Cambridge: Harvard-USAID.

Street Children and Marginalized Population Work Needs

UNA-USA. 1988. *A Successor Vision: The United Nations of Tomorrow*. United Nations Association of the United States of America.
UNICEF. 1984. Abandoned Children—What Can Be Done? Urban Examples for Basic Service Development in Cities. *E* 7 (April).
—. 1988. *The State of the World's Children*. Oxford: Oxford University Press.
Myers, William. 1988. Promoting Alternative Services for Street Children: A Case Study of National Mobilization (Recent Case Based on FUNABEM, manuscript forthcoming). Brazil: ILO.
For general information on work and employment programs, see ILO *Bibliography of Published Research on World Employment Program* (current edition, 6th).

Chapters Four and Five: Education Technology

Anzalone, Stephen. (no date). *An Evaluation of the Effects of Computer-Assisted Instruction on Student Achievement in Grenada.* Washington, D.C.: U.S. Agency for International Development.

Anzalone, Stephen. (no date). *Using Instructional Hardware for Primary Education in Developing Countries: A Review of the Literature.* Cambridge, MA: Project BRIDGES, Harvard University Institute for International Development.

Arena, Eduardo. 1988. *The Mexican Telesecundaria System: A Cost Analysis.* Ottawa: International Development Research Centre.

Block, Clifford, Julianne Gilmore, Carlos Mora and Stephen Anzalone. 1987. Computers in Classrooms in LDC's: Strategies and an Update on Some Work in Progress. Washington, D.C.: Comparative and International Education Society, 31st Annual Meeting, Discussion Panel.

Castro, Claudio de Moura. Computing Costs of Instruction: A Lotus 123 Template. Mimeo.

CD-I News. 1987. *Link Resources Corp.* 1 (12):4 (Oct). New York: Emerging Technologies Publications.

Clearinghouse on Development Communication. 1986. *Project Profiles.* Washington, D.C.: U.S. Agency for International Development.

Cuban, Larry. 1986. *Teachers and Machines: The Classroom Use of Technology Since 1920.* New York: Teachers College Press, Columbia University.

Danrey, Jean. 1988. *The Use of Computer-Assisted Instruction in a University Center for Adult Training: The Case of the Centre Universite—Economie d'Education Permanente (CUEEP) of Lille, France* (Unpublished paper). Dijon, France: University of Bourgogne.

—.1985-1987. *Development Communication Report* (various issues). Washington, D.C.: Clearinghouse on Development Communication.

Ely, Donald P. and Tjeerd Plomp. 1986. The Promises of Educational Technology: A Reassessment. *International Review of Education,* 32 (3): 231-249.

Friend, Jamesine. 1985. *Classroom Uses of the Computer: A Retrospective View with Implications for Developing Countries.*

Washington, D.C.: World Bank Discussion Paper (Nov.), Education and Training Series Report No. EDT10.

—. 1987. *Planning Ahead for Large-Scale Success.* Shelby, NC: Friend Dialogues Technical Report No. 703. (Aug.).

Fuller, Bruce. 1985. *Raising School Quality in Developing Countries: What Investments Boost Learning?* Washington, D.C.: World Bank Discussion Paper (Sept.), Education and Training Series Report No. EDT7.

Goldschmidt, Douglas. 1987. *An Analysis of the Costs and Revenues of Rural Telecommunications Systems.* Washington, D.C.: U.S. Agency for International Development.

Hawkridge, David and Bob McCormick. 1983. China's Television Universities. *British Journal of Educational Technology,* 14 (3): 168-173 (Oct).

Herschbach, Dennis R. 1984. *Addressing Vocational Training and Retraining Through Educational Technology: Policy Alternatives.* Columbus, OH: The National Center for Research in Vocational Education, Ohio State University.

—. 1984. *Vocational Planning for Developing Countries: Curricular and Educational Technology Alternatives.* Washington, D.C.: U.S. Agency for International Development.

Hershfield, A.E. 1982. Developing Technology to Enhance the Educational Process. *Technology and Educational Policy Implementation Evaluation.* Washington, D.C.: The Institute for Educational Leadership.

Kamata, Hiroko. 1987. Vocational Education and Use of Computers in Japan. Mimeo.

Levin, Henry M., Gene V. Glass and Gail R. Meister. 1987. Cost-Effectiveness of Computer-Assisted Instruction. *Evaluation Review* 11 (1): 58-72 (Feb).

Lipson, J.I. 1981. Changing Organizational Structures to Capitalize on Technology. *Technology and Educational Policy Implementation Evaluation.* Washington, D.C.: The Institute for Educational Leadership.

Lockheed, Marlaine E. 1985 (1). *Determinants of Student Computer Use: An Analysis of Data From the 1984 National Assessment of Educational Progress.* Princeton, NJ: Educational Testing Service.

—. 1985 (2). Women, Girls and Computers: A First Look at the Evidence. *Sex Roles* 13: 115-122.

—, and Ellen B. Mandinach. 1986. *Trends in Educational Computing: Decreasing Interest and the Changing Focus of Instruction.* Washington, D.C.: World Bank Reprint Series 377.

—, S. Vail and B. Fuller. 1987. How Textbooks Affect Achievement in Developing Countries: Evidence from Thailand. *Educational Evaluation and Policy Analysis* 18 (4): 379-392.

—, and Eric Hanushek. 1988. Improving Educational Efficiency in Developing Countries: What Do We Know? *Compare* 18 (1): 21-38.

Makau, B.M. 1988. *New Information Technology and Quality Education: The Potential and Problems of Computers in Schools.* Washington, D.C.: World Bank Workshop on the Aga Khan Foundation Computers in Education Project in Kenya, April 18-29.

McLellan, Iain. 1986. *Television for Development: The African Experience.* Ottawa: International Development Research Centre Manuscript Report.

Medrano, Luis E. 1987. *Peru Rural Communications Services Project: Final Field Report.* Washington, D.C.: U.S. Agency for International Development.

Oliveira, Joao Batista Araujo. 1988. *Computer Education in Developing Countries: Facing Hard Choices.* Unpublished paper.

—, and Francois Orivel. Forthcoming. Training Teachers at a Distance: The Case of LOGOS II in Brazil. In Stromquist, Nelly, ed. *Adoption and Institutionalization of Educational Innovation.*

Orivel, Francois. 1982. *Preparation of a Proposed World Bank Education Project in China: Television University and Short-Term Vocational Colleges—Economic Justification* (Unpublished paper). Dijon, France: University of Bourgogne.

—. 1987. *Costs and Effectiveness of Distance Teaching Systems: A Methodological Approach* (Unpublished paper). Dijon, France: University of Bourgogne.

—. *Prospects: Quarterly Review of Education. 1988.* 17 (3). Paris: UNESCO.

Psacharopoulos, George and Maureen Woodhall. 1985. *Education for Development: An Analysis of Investment Choices.* New York: Oxford University Press.

—. *Radio Learning.* 1988. 2 (Apr). Washington, D.C.: U.S. Agency for International Development.

Ruth, Stephen R. and Charles K. Mann, eds. 1987. *Microcomputers in Public Policy: Applications for Developing Countries*. Boulder, CO: Westview Press for the American Association for the Advancement of Science, AAAS Selected Symposium 102.

Schramm, W. 1977. *Big Media, Little Media*. Beverly Hills, CA: Sage Publications.

Sharma, Motilal. 1988 (1). *Development of Education in Asia and the Pacific*. Manila: Asian Development Bank, Panel Review Meeting, Regional Technical Assistance, March 14-15.

—. 1988 (2) *Technologies to Improve In-Class Instruction* (Resource Paper). Seminar on Using Technologies for Education and Training: An Economic Perspective, April 18-29. Washington, D.C.: The World Bank.

Shaw, Willard D. 1987. *Distance Education Via Satellite: A Case Study of the Indonesian Distance Education Satellite System*. Washington, D.C.: U.S. Agency for International Development.

Shepperd, Richard E. *Simulation and Learning Efficiency*. (Unpublished paper).

Stahmer, Anna and Gerald Lalor. 1987. *The University of the West Indies Distance Teaching Experiment: A Case Study*. Washington, D.C.: U.S. Agency for International Development.

Thiagarajan, Sivasailam and Aida L. Pasigna. 1987. *Using Soft Technologies of Learning for Primary Education in Developing Countries: A Review of the Literature*. Cambridge, MA: Project BRIDGES, Harvard University Institute for International Development.

Tiene, Drew and Shigenari Futagami. 1987. *Educational Media in Retrospect*. Education and Training Series Report No. EDT58. Washington, D.C.: World Bank Discussion Paper.

Tietjen, Karen. 1987 (1). *The AID Rural Satellite Program: An Overview*. Washington, D.C.: U.S. Agency for International Development.

—. 1987 (2). *The AID Rural Satellite Program: Executive Summary*. Washington, D.C.: U.S. Agency for International Development.

Wagner, L. 1982. *The Economics of Educational Media*. New York: St. Martin's Press.

Woolery, Arlo and Sharon Shea, eds. 1985. *Introduction to Computer Assisted Valuation*. Boston, MA: Oelgeschlager, Gunn & Hain in association with the Lincoln Institute of Land Policy.

ANNEXES

ANNEX I
Policy Survey

This annex reports the results of a policy survey conducted by EDC in order to include the broad participation of a larger group of researchers, policy-makers and planners in the findings of this report. Questions were elicited from a group of experts and practitioners in an initial planning meeting for this study and two survey instruments were prepared (one each for education and training) to explore the issues, define the problems and consider alternative policy options for future needs for international technical co-operation in education and training. The results of the survey are based on the responses of 100 returns representing 33 countries. This annex provides a review of the methodology, the most striking policy statements, an analysis of the basic data and a full summary of the data.

I.A Methodology

A total of 353 questionnaires were mailed to policy and planning experts and practitioners in 45 countries. Participants were chosen from lists of researchers, policy-makers and planners in the fields of education and training. The survey questionnaires were designed to assess the relative levels of the needs and strategies for education and training in developing countries. The Education and Training Surveys each presented a series of policy and planning statements and options that were organized in twelve groups. Participants were asked to rank option statements in their order of importance.

Questionnaires were mailed on 24 June 1988 with the request that participants return them promptly. Survey responses received after 15 August 1988 were not included in the data analysis. Responses were received from participants of both developed and developing country nationalities from countries (including international organizations headquartered there) in the following geographical breakdown: Training: 41 per cent USA and Canada; 14 per cent Europe; 45 per cent developing countries; Education: 43 per cent USA and Canada; 2 per cent Europe; 55 per cent developing countries. Over 40 questionnaires could either not be properly delivered or were replied to after the deadline.

replied to after the deadline.

Survey responses were entered into an Excel spreadsheet model. Averages and standard deviation were calculated on the aggregated data to determine the average ranking of priorities. Data was then disaggregated into four groups which were classified as Governmental, Non-Governmental, LDC-Specific and LDC-General. These groups were determined by the demographic information supplied by each respondent. Surveys categorized as governmental included those individuals who indicated current positions with a ministry of education or with a government agency such as USAID. Non-Governmental affiliations included independent consultants and university researchers. The LDC-S category (Less Developed Country-Specific) included those individuals who indicated a specific country context within which their responses were given. LDC-General included those who indicated that their responses were given within the broad context of developing countries in general. Figures 1 and 2 below present the responses by category for both questionnaires.

Figure 1: Education Survey Responses by Category N = 49

Figure 2: Training Survey Responses by Category N = 51

Non-Government N = 35(71%)	Government N = 14(29%)	Non-Government Gov't N = 36 (71%)	Government N = 15(29%)
LDC-General N = 24 (49%)	LDC-Specific N = 25 (51%)	LDC-General LDC N = 28 (55%)	LDC-Specific N = 23 (45%)

The figures reported for both surveys are based on responses from all individuals who returned the survey. However, not all individuals responded to every policy option. Since the total number of respondents in the Education Survey is 49, then if an N of 42 is reported for one question, then 7 individuals did not answer that question. Some individuals judged a question either beyond their competence or unclear; in such a case the individual would not respond to that option or group of options.

Averages were calculated for each of the categories of disaggregated data in order to compare priorities across the four groups. Based on the averages, the top three statement options were selected for each of the five data groups: (1) Total Average, (2) LDC-S, (3) LDC-G, (4) NGO, and (5) Governmental Organizations. A general descriptive analysis was then prepared to present a broad view of the trends, options and priorities for determining the future needs for international technical cooperation in training as indicated by the survey results.

I.B Trends in Education and Training: Salient Policy Statements from the Survey Results

The following statements are derived from the policy survey:

- The primary goals for training and development are employment generation and economic development.
- Highest priority toward investments in primary and vocational education.
- Investments in university education will be given lowest priority.
- Emphasis will be placed on the satisfaction of manpower requirements and the provision of skills for job creation and entrepreneurial purposes.
- Training needs for industrial development will focus on small and medium-size enterprises.
- Teacher training deserves priority attention to increase the quality of education in all sectors.
- Greater concern for local context and increased emphasis on decentralized planning and increased participation at regional and local levels.
- Radio and microcomputers rank equal and highest among the hard technologies for their impact on teaching and learning, but priority will still be given to the broad use of educational technologies, including soft technology, or "appropriate technologies."
- Short-term, in-country training and technical problem solving and analysis are the formats in which technical assistance is most useful.
- Long-term relations established between providers and receivers.

- Agricultural and rural development needs to receive increased attention.
- Need for more activity to address school health issues to be predicated upon research and data collecting.

Survey results indicate that there is broad agreement with the description and analysis presented in this paper. Analysis was first completed using averages based on aggregated data. However, the analysis of disaggregated data revealed some differences among the four groups: Government and Non-Governmental (NGO) affiliates, Less Developed Countries—General (LDC-G), and Less Developed Country (or region)—Specific (LDC-S). For example, both Government and LDC-General groups gave top priority to investment in primary education and vocational education, while the LDC-Specific group indicated a preference for primary and secondary education over vocational education.

Response to options offered in the category of cost and constraint trends also evidenced some disagreement among groups. On average the NGO and LDC-G groups ranked inadequate supply of trained vocational teachers first priority, while the LDC-S and Government groups ranked inadequate supply of trained vocational teachers third and fourth place respectively.

When asked to prioritize the uses of modern equipment, the NGO category showed less optimism about the use of educational technology in learning, whereas the LDC-G group ranked the uses of computers, TV and radio a higher priority in general than other groups.

The diversity of opinion expressed in this general survey report identifies a need for further study to explore the specific points of reference of the different respondent groups in order to clarify policy options for future needs for international technical co-operation in education and training.

I.C Basic Data Analysis: Education Survey

Investments in Education
The survey asked respondents to rank in terms of priority where investments should be made in the education sector. The five choices were: a) primary education, b) secondary education, c)

university education, d) non-formal education and e) other. Average response indicated that investment priorities in education should be made in: (1) primary, (2) secondary, (3) non-formal, (4) other and (5) university. Thirty-five per cent of all responses indicated a preference for the "other" category, 61 per cent of which favored vocational education. On average, those who wrote in vocational education ranked it (3), giving it priority over non-formal and university education. However, within the broad category of LDC-General, vocational education ranked second to primary education. University education ranked lowest priority across all groups.

Although total averaged out responses yielded the above ranking, disaggregated groupings indicated varied priorities. When vocational education was calculated as a category, the results from respondent data among both the Government and LDC-General groups yielded the following prioritization: (1) primary education, (2) vocational education, (3) secondary education, (4) non-formal education, (5) university education. Among the LDC-Specific group vocational education ranked (4) after primary, secondary and non-formal education. These results indicate a trend toward greater investment priorities in primary education and vocational education.

Primary Education
Problems: Survey results show that on average across all respondent groups the top three problems deserving priority attention in education at the primary level are: (1) teacher quality, (2) insufficient education materials and, (3) inadequate facilities. Lack of jobs was of lowest concern and, surprisingly enough, costs rated second lowest.
Interventions: As for priority interventions in primary education, respondents ranked the following among the first three choices: (1) teacher training, (2) textbooks and materials production, (3) educational planning and analysis. School health ranked lowest priority.
Curriculum design: Although respondents did not rate inadequate curriculum as a high priority in primary education, when asked to rank the major problems or needs related to curriculum design the following rankings were given: (1) too oriented to rote learning, (2) not geared to practical life needs, (3) too geared to examination system, (4) not geared to student ability and (5)

inappropriate materials. Strategies to address problems in curriculum design were ranked on average as follows: (1) train teachers to make better use of curriculum, (2) develop improved materials, (3) give training to upgrade design skills, and (4) tie curriculum design to student assessment.

Secondary Education
Problems: Response across groups was mixed as to priority problems and interventions in secondary education. On average, the ranking was as follows: (1) teacher quality, (2) inadequate curriculum, (3) insufficient educational materials, with lowest ranking given to costs. However, the average respondent in the LDC-Specific category indicated that lack of jobs was the second major problem in secondary education.
Interventions: Interventions were prioritized as follows: (1) educational planning & analysis, (2) textbooks and materials production, (3) teacher training. Those categorized as Government showed some preference for teacher training over textbooks and materials production, but otherwise all other groups were in agreement with the priorities expressed by the total average.
Curriculum design: Problems/needs in curriculum design in secondary education were rated as follows: (1) not geared to practical life needs, (2) too geared to examination system, (3) too oriented to rote learning, (4) not geared to student ability and (5) inappropriate materials. To address problems in curriculum design in secondary education, the following strategies were ranked: (1) develop improved materials, (2) train teachers to make better use of curriculum, (3) tie curriculum to student assessment and (4) train to upgrade design.

Higher Education
Problems: Higher education problems were prioritized in the following order: (1) teacher quality, (2) inadequate curriculum, (3) cost. Teacher quantity was ranked lowest priority. This was not true of all groups, however. Lack of access took fourth priority on average, but placed much higher in three disaggregated groupings. Government respondents prioritized lack of access as the first problem with costs in second place and followed by teacher quality and inadequate curriculum. The LDC-Specific category ranked inadequate curriculum first, followed by costs,

inadequate curriculum and lack of access, while the LDC-General category ranked lack of access second to teacher quality.

Interventions: The priority intervention across all groups was (1) educational planning & analysis. Other averages ranked as follows: (2) textbooks and materials production, (3) teacher training, (4) curriculum design; (5) school health received the lowest priority. LDC-Specific group ranked teacher training second, followed by textbooks & materials production (3). Curriculum design ranked third for Non-Government and LDC-General groups.

Curriculum design: The needs related to curriculum design were prioritized as follows: (1) too geared to examination system, (2) not geared to practical life needs, (3) too oriented to rote learning. Strategies to improve curriculum design were prioritized as follows: (1) develop improved materials, (2) train teachers to make better use of curriculum, (3) tie to student assessment.

Non-Formal education

Problems: Priorities in non-formal education were ranked on average as (1) inadequate curriculum, (2) teacher quality, (3) insufficient educational materials. However, insufficient educational materials ranked first priority by both the LDC-General and Governmental groups. LDC-Specific group ranked teacher quality as the first problem.

Intervention: Educational planning and analysis ranked first priority intervention followed by teacher training, curriculum design. School health ranked lowest overall. Curriculum design received first preference ranking in the LDC-General group and second priority among the Government Group, whereas teacher training received first priority by the Non-Govt. group.

Curriculum design: Needs related to curriculum design in non-formal education were rated: (1) not geared to practical needs, (2) not geared to student abilities, (3) inappropriate materials. Strategies to address problems in curriculum design in non-formal education were ranked: (1) develop improved materials, (2) train teachers to make better use, (3) tie curriculum to student assessment.

Facilities planning and construction

Problems: The major problems related to facilities planning and construction were ranked as follows: (1) inadequate equipment &

materials, (2) insufficient maintenance, (3) lack of classroom space.
Interventions: The strategies to improve facilities and construction were ranked as follows: (1) greater community participation in school construction & maintenance, (2) funds for purchase of materials and equipment, (3) modifying school calendar to maximize use of existing facilities. Lowest ranking was given to greater reliance on private sector and the training of architects.

Textbooks and materials production
Problems: The major problems/needs related to textbooks and materials production were rated as: (1) lack of design and production know-how, (2) inadequate curriculum, (3) lack of printing & publishing facilities; lowest priority was given to lack of private sector investment.
Interventions: To address the problems there was overall agreement on the following priorities: (1) training in textbook design and production, (2) greater investment in printing/publishing plants, equipment and paper supplies and (3) greater privatization of the textbook/materials design/production function. Lowest ranking was given to shift to non-print media.

Educational planning and analysis
Problems: The major problems and needs in educational planning and analysis were ranked across all groups as: (1) human resource planning, (2) organizational systems, (3) management information systems, and (4) financial planning. There was some variation in agreement to this average overall ranking. Government Group average ranked organizational systems first, followed by human resource planning and management information systems. LDC-General ranked financial planning second to human resource planning followed by organizational systems and management information systems.
Interventions: To address these problems, respondents across all groups agreed on the ranking of strategies as follows: (1) planning and analytical skills training, (2) decentralization of planning and (3) greater investment in data processing facilities.

Teachers
Problems: The problems/needs related to teachers were ranked as follows: (1) salaries and incentives, (2) selection and recruitment,

(3) pre-service training; lowest rank was given to the high percent of budget spent on teachers.

Interventions: To address problems related to teachers, the following ranks were given to strategies: (1) strengthening of finance & incentives support, (2) improved in-service training, (3) improved pre-service training. The choices receiving lowest ranking were: to give teachers more autonomy; reduce dependence through alternative delivery.

Techniques for Improving Instruction: To improve instruction, the following techniques were given the following rating on average: (1) diagnostic/prescriptive instruction, (2) mastery learning, (3) individualized instruction. However, both LDC-Specific and the Non-Gov't groups ranked individualized instruction second after diagnostic/prescriptive instruction.

Testing and Evaluation: Problems related to testing and evaluation were rated as follows: (1) lack of assessment procedures to diagnose, (2) lack of accountability of student performance, (3) lack of appropriate grade and subject matter exams. Strategies to address problems related to testing and evaluation were rated as follows: (1) increase teacher assessment skills, (2) introduce grade-level reference tests, (3) develop standardized achievement tests. This average rating was true across all groups except that the Government Group gave a second place rating to the development of standardized achievement tests.

School Health

Although school health was not given priority among respondents when listed with policy option choices in other parts of the questionnaire, when asked to address the issue directly, 42 respondents answered that they lacked knowledge about the problem. The major problems/needs related to school health were ranked: (1) lack of data on extent of school health problems and their effect on learning, (2) insufficient school health facilities, (3) inappropriate school feeding programmes and policies, and (4) lack of school health standards.

The ways to address problems related to school health were ranked: (1) strengthening of school health facilities, (2) epidemiological research into school health problems, (3) enactment of national school health standards.

I.D Basic Data Analysis: Training

The Primary Goals for Training and Development
The survey asked respondents to rank in terms of priority the primary goals for training and development. Twelve options were given. Across all groups, the top three rankings were: (1) employment generation; (2) training primarily for economic development, and; (3) increased quality of training. The Government and LDC-General groups rated both employment generation and training primarily for economic development top priority, bringing increased quality of training to second priority and shift of public resources from academic education to vocational training to third priority placement. Overall averages indicate, however, the option for the shift of public resources from academic education to vocational training placed fourth priority, followed by (5) increased opportunities for women and (6) requirement of teacher certification exams.

The following options were given least priority on average: (7) national certification programme established for various levels of workers; (8) industry to provide teacher training; (9) substantial increases in teacher salaries; (10) national competency exams required for all students; and (11) training health workers considered a good investment.

There were some differences in priorities in the disaggregated groups. Increased opportunities for women was ranked fourth priority by the LDC-G group, whereas the NGOs ranked it sixth priority as did the LDC-S group. The option for industry to provide teacher training ranked fourth priority for the Gov't group, whereas it was ranked lowest by the NGO and LDC-G groups.

There were 12 responses given in the "other" option, four of which referred to ways in which to increase the quality of training through improved facilities and equipment; three individuals referred to kinds of employment generation through self-employment training and micro-enterprise development; three individuals referred to the need for training for rural communities in particular.

The Basis for Planning, Analysis and Assessment of the Training System
Priority options for the bases for planning, analysis and

assessment of the training system were ranked as follows: (1) satisfaction of manpower requirements; (2) concentration on training programmes that are justified by labor market information; (3) provision of skills for job creation and entrepreneurial purposes; and (4) creation of national policy committees to allocate education and training resources. Options ranking in the mid-range included (5) creation of an administrative structure for all education and training; (6) provision of skills only for jobs that already exist; and (7) priority for short-term training of adults for the work force over basic education for youth. The lowest ranking priorities were: (8) provision of computerized management information on the work force in every country; and (9) highly centralized training, policy and funding.

The most notable exception to this order was received from the LDC-Specific group that gave equal ranking in (5) fifth place to short-term training of adults for the work force over basic education for youth priority and (5) creation of an administrative structure for all education and training.

Cost and Constraint Trends
Among 10 options that the questionnaire offered in the category of cost and constraint trends, the following priorities received top ranking: (1) inadequate supply of trained vocational teachers and cost as a major factor limiting programme development shared first priority; (2) the lack of financial resources; and (3) the lack of instructional materials and equipment. Mid-range ranking was given to the following options: (4) lack of private industry support for the cost of training; (5) lack of use of educational technology to reduce training cost; (6) poor classroom management practices. Lowest priority rankings were given to the following options: (7) vocational education to be considered a terminal education, with completers not permitted to go on to college; (8) lack of PVO participation in training programmes; and (9) institutional training facilities not fully utilized.

There were some notable exceptions to the average priority rankings. On average the NGO and LDC-G groups ranked inadequate supply of trained vocational teachers first priority while the LDC-S and Government groups ranked inadequate supply of trained vocational teachers third and fourth place respectively.

The ranking for PVO participation was hindered due to the fact that people did not understand the meaning of the PVO term. Two individuals asked: "What is a PVO?" Two individuals commented on the fact that technical education is perceived as second class. "It is better to have a Ph.D. and be unemployed," wrote one respondent.

Uses of Modern Equipment and Pedagogy
When asked to prioritize the uses of modern equipment and pedagogy, the average ranking among 10 options was as follows: (1) educational technology generally; (2) educational technology to offset the lack of trained teachers; (3) computers as a major instructional tool; (4) educational technology to double the amount of learning; (5) knowledge of computer usage by every student and TV to become an excellent way to provide training; (6) radio as an effective way to deliver training; (7) satellite TV as a major means of delivery of training in developing countries; and (8) minicomputers to deliver up to half or more of the training.

Exceptions to the average rankings were noted in the LDC-G group where the uses of computers, TV and radio were given higher priority and ranked closely together; the use of TV and computers shared fourth priority ranking followed by radio in fifth place. The NGO category showed less optimism about the use of educational technology in learning, ranking educational technology to double the amount of learning in sixth place.

Half of the comments written in this category (7 out of 40 total responses) referred to the level of technology: "appropriate technology, not just high tech," "basics are the most needed, *not* modern equipment," and "distance learning with appropriate technology" were statements made in this category.

Training Needs for Industrial Development
Individuals responded to seven options offered in this category by prioritizing the following rank order: (1) small and medium size enterprises, (2) small enterprises, (3) employment requiring high level training, (4) rural areas, (5) urban areas and (6) large enterprises. This ranking was true across all groups with one exception: the LDC-S group ranked the need for industrial development rural areas second, with small and medium size enterprises and small enterprises ranked equally in first place.

Agriculture and Rural Needs
The questionnaire asked individuals to rank three statements on agriculture and rural needs in terms of accuracy with the following results: (1) greater emphasis on training for rural development; (2) training focus on agriculture sector; (3) training in the agricultural sector more important than training for industrial sector. This ranking was agreed across all groups.

Training in the Formal and Informal Sectors
The questionnaire responses revealed that equal priority must be given for training in the formal and informal sectors. When asked to prioritize the order of importance on the emphasis directed toward training for the (1) formal sector and (2) informal sector, the ranking was split evenly among all groups. Two individuals commented: "Absolutely depends upon local employment conditions" and "Both are important but the formal sector is more able to provide training; the informal sector *needs more help.*"

Policy Options
In this category, fourteen policy options were offered for prioritization with the following top rankings resulting: (1) most training programmes to combine training with work experience; (2) formal training to provide specific skill training just prior to job entry; (3) retraining and upgrading to be more important than initial skill development; (4) most training to take place in industry. Mid-range rankings were given to the following options: (5) all training and training materials to be competency based; (6) formal training to be given for high level jobs; low level jobs taught on the job; (7) teachers to be trained through in-service programmes; (8) emphasis placed on training foremen and supervisors as trainers of their employees; (9) training to be taken out of school and carried out at the work site. Lowest rankings were given to: (10) all secondary schools to offer diversified vocational training programmes; (11) regionalized development of instructional materials; (12) national training systems to be decentralized; (13) apprenticeship to be the primary method used for training; (14) the responsibility for vocational training to be shifted to ministries of labor.

The Needs for Technical Co-operation
The needs for technical co-operation were ranked among five options as follows: (1) facilitating policy for training; (2) evaluation of training policies, implementation and outcomes; (3) establishing data bases related to training needs and outputs; and (4) curriculum development. This ranking order was agreed upon across all groups with one exception. The LDC-S group gave first priority to establishing data bases related to training needs and outputs.

The Format Where Technical Assistance and Training in Education Are Most Useful
Technical assistance and training in education are regarded as most useful in formats ranked in the following order: (1) short-term, in-country training; (2) technical problem solving and analysis; (3) project design and evaluation; (4) short-term overseas training; (5) policy dialogue; and (6) long-term overseas training.

Rank order of priorities differed across groups. The NGO group ranked technical problem solving and analysis and project design and evaluation in first place followed by short-term, in-country training and short-term overseas training; the LDC-S group placed technical problem solving and analysis third. Greatest disagreement with the aggregated averages was observed in the Government group. This group agreed that short-term, in-country training was first priority but the following priority rankings were radically different from other groups as follows: (2) short-term overseas training; (3) policy dialogue; (4) long-term overseas training; (5) project design and evaluation; (6) technical problem solving and analysis.

Comments on these options noted that the format for technical assistance is dependent on context, on the "type of programme," or that the format "may vary with the situation. In some cases there is no facility, equipment or instructional material available." One individual responded: "These can't be ranked unless one knows the specific purpose of the activity. They are all important and of top priority depending on the activity."

The Delivery of Technical Assistance
The problems related to delivery of technical assistance were ranked by those answering the training survey as follows: (1) lack

of long-term linkages between providers and receivers; (2) lack of understanding of local context; (3) assistance is provided without transferring technical know-how; (4) time horizon of intervention is too short; (5) assumes western model of development. This ranking was agreed upon across all groups, with one exception. The average Government response ranked lack of understanding of local context in first position and lack of long-term linkages between providers and receivers in third place.

Comments given by eight individuals in the "other" category made note of the problems that poor management and mismanagement create for the delivery of technical assistance. Problems also were noted in the maintenance of the training equipment. "After launching the project, the equipment has been left unattended. Either it is still operational for training or it is obsolete. Technical assistance is thorough, but the assessment/evaluation of training equipment is neglected."

Those answering the same question on the education survey gave higher ratings to the problems associated with the lack of understanding of the local context and the assumption of the western model of development. The top three problems related to the delivery of technical assistance in education were selected and ranked by those in the education sector as follows: (1) lack of understanding of the local context; (2) lack of long-term linkages between providers and receivers; (3) assumption of the western model of development.

I.E Basic Data Analysis: Technology

The Use of Educational Technologies
The following rankings were given to problems related to the use of educational technologies: (1) lack of knowledge about the use of specific technologies; (2) lack of technical know-how; (3) high capital costs. Technology perceived as a threat was given the lowest ranking. Each group, however, rated the first three in different order. On average, the Government category rated high capital costs as the second major problem, while the non-government category rated lack of technical know-how the first problem, followed by lack of knowledge about use of specific technologies second, and high capital costs third. LDC-Specific category rated lack of technical know-how first, capital costs

third. The two other choices — lack of adequate repair and maintenance services, and lack of physical infrastructure — rated somewhere inthe middle and were lost in the averaging between the top three and the lowest choices, but fell very close between.

Ranking ways to address problems related to the use of educational technologies, the following priorities were given by the respondents: (1) training to increase technical know-how; (2) small pilot projects to demonstrate feasibility; (3) training to increase national awareness of the potential of various technologies. Government incentives to entrepreneurs received the lowest ranking.

The Impact of Technologies on Teaching and Learning
Among eight possible choices, the technologies selected for their impact on teaching and learning were: (1) microcomputers and radio received equal ranking for first priority; (2) video cassette recorders; (3) television; satellite communications received the lowest overall ranking. However, the average non-government response indicated that television and microcomputers were first priority followed by radio and video cassette recorders, while radio was first choice among LDC-General.

Comments by several respondents indicated that the question was too broad and suggested that the impact of technology on teaching and learning depends on what is being taught and at what level, and is dependent on specific geographic regions. One respondent stated, "distance teaching via radio is suitable in Africa, while microcomputers are useful at the university level and satellite communications are useful in Asia."

Uses of Modern Equipment and Pedagogy
When asked to prioritize the uses of modern equipment and pedagogy, the average ranking among 10 options was as follows: (1) educational technology generally; (2) educational technology to off-set the lack of trained teachers; (3) computers as a major instructional tool; (4) educational technology to double the amount of learning; (5) knowledge of computer usage by every student and TV to become an excellent way to provide training; (6) radio as an effective way to deliver training; (7) satellite TV as a major means of delivery of training in developing countries; and (8) minicomputers to deliver up to half or more of the training.

Exceptions to the average rankings were noted in the LDC-G

group where the uses of computers, TV and radio were given higher priority and ranked closely together; the use of TV and computers shared fourth priority ranking followed by radio in fifth place. The NGO category showed less optimism about the use of educational technology in learning, ranking educational technology to double the amount of learning in sixth place.

Half of the comments written in this category (7 out of 40 total responses) referred to the level of technology: "appropriate technology, not just high tech," "basics are the most needed, *not* modern equipment," and "distance learning with appropriate technology" were statements made in this category.

I.F Basic Data Analysis: Technology Assistance

Technical Assistance Requirements for Training and Development
Respondents ranked three options offered in technical assistance requirements for training and development as follows: (1) technical co-operation to analyze retaining needs; (2) a greater reliance on UN agencies to analyze, design and assist in implementing training programmes; and, also ranking in second place, (2) less use of external experts; national experts should provide most of the support services needed for programme development.

However, the LDC-S and Government groups indicated first priority to less use of external experts; national experts should provide most of the support services needed for programme development. These two groups also indicated lowest priority to greater reliance on UN agencies to analyze, design and assist in implementing training programmes.

Nine individuals (19 per cent of the total responses) indicated first priority ranking policy options in the "other" category. Responses in this category indicate a preference for a total systems approach to technical assistance, a focus on local capabilities and needs. Written responses with reference to a total systems approach included: "A total effort:" UNDP, World Bank, Asian Bank, in-country support, etc.; "international co-operation with internal and external experts working together through a multitude of network organization." Other responses referring to local needs included: "Local capability to determine training needs to be upgraded," and "Again, depends upon local needs."

The Format Where Technical Assistance and Training in Education Are Most Useful

Technical assistance and training in education are regarded by trainers as most useful in formats ranked in the following order: (1) short-term, in-country training; (2) technical problem-solving and analysis; (3) project design and evaluation; (4) short-term overseas training; (5) policy dialogue; and (6) long-term training.

Rank order of priorities differed across groups. The NGO group ranked technical problem solving and analysis and project design and evaluation in first place followed by short-term, in-country training and short-term overseas training; the LDC-S group placed technical problem-solving and analysis third. Greatest disagreement with the aggregated averages was observed in the Government group. This group agreed that short-term, in-country training was first priority but the following priority rankings were radically different from other groups as follows: (2) short-term overseas training; (3) policy dialogue; (4) long-term overseas training; (5) project design and evaluation; (6) technical problem solving and analysis.

Comments on these options noted that the format for technical assistance is dependent on context, on the "type of programme," or that "the format may vary with the situation. In some cases there is no facility, equipment or instructional material available." One individual responded: "These can't be ranked unless one knows the specific purpose of the activity. They are all important and of top priority depending on the activity."

ANNEX I: DATA SUMMARY
Summary: Education Survey Results

	Average Rating				Standard	
	Total	Gov't	Non-Gov't	LDC-S	LDC-G	Deviation	N

1. Rank in terms of priority where investments should be made in the education sector: (5 categories)

	Total	Gov't	Non-Gov't	LDC-S	LDC-G	Dev.	N
1. primary education	1.6	1	1.8	1.5	1.6	1.0	49
2. secondary education	2.5	2.6	2.5	2.6	2.4	1.0	48
3. non-formal education	2.7	2.8	2.7	2.6	2.8	1.1	42
4. other	3.3	2.7	3.4	3.3	2.8	1.4	18
vocational	2.6	2.5	3.0	3.0	2.4	1.4	11
5. university education	3.5	3.9	3.4	3.7	3.4	1.1	47

Other:
- vocational-technical
- Education for women
- vocational education
- upgrading professionals
- vocational
- cultural
- education for disabled
- craft design and technology education for primary, secondary and non-formal education
- pre-vocational
- literacy programs
- vocational training system
- distance education
- preschool education
- technical education
- technical & vocational education
- project related training

Comments: Secondary education on selective basis, for skills training.

	Average Rating					Standard	
	Total	Gov't	Non-Gov't	LDC-S	LDC-G	Deviation	N

2.1. Rank in terms of priority what are the major problems within primary education: (11 choices)

1. teacher quality	2.8	3.2	2.9	2.1	3.5	2.1	47
2. other	3.3	1	3.8	7.0	1.5	3.9	6
3. insufficient education materials	3.6	2.5	4.2	3.7	3.5	2.3	43
4. inadequate facilities	3.9	3.4	4.0	3.6	4.3	2.4	35
5. lack of jobs	7.8	7.2	8.0	6.3	6.3	2.6	28
6. cost	6.3	6.3	6.5	6.3	6.3	2.6	28

Other:
- subsidies for materials and textbooks
- Lack of textbooks
- population policy
- lack of access by females/rural poor
- Active method

2.2. Major problems in secondary education: (11 choices)

1. teacher quality	2.9	2.7	3.2	2.6	3.2	2.3	27
2. inadequate curriculum	4.3	3.6	4.5	4.5	4.1	2.4	22
3. insufficient educational materials	4.4	3.4	4.9	4.6	4.3	2.5	21
4. lack of jobs	4.8	3.8	5.5	4.3	5.3	3.4	16
5. cost	6.1	4.7	6.7	6.9	5.1	4.4	17

Note: on selective basis, for skills training

2.3 Major problems in higher education: (11 choices)

1. teacher quality	3.1	3	3.1	5.4	3.6	2.5	19
2. inadequate curriculum	3.6	3	3.6	3.4	3.7	2.2	16
3. cost	4.1	2.3	4.9	4.6	3.8	3.1	15
4. lack of access	4.6	1.7	5.5	5.4	3.6	3.2	17
5. teacher quantity	5.9	4.5	6.2	5.0	6.7	2.8	13

2.4 Major problems in non-formal education: (11 choices)

1. inadequate curriculum	3.1	3	3.1	3.6	2.6	1.5	16
2. teacher quality	3.5	3.7	3.5	3.1	3.8	2.0	17
3. insufficient educational materials	3.9	2.3	4.6	4.8	3.1	2.8	16

	Average Rating					Standard	
	Total	Gov't	Non-Gov't	LDC-S	LDC-G	Deviation	N

Other General Comments on 2.1-2.4:

- cost to parent, or opportunities lost
- lack of attention to segment who needs it
- increase the cooperation among agencies concerned
- low government priority for rural population
- shortage of funds/growing population
- subsidies for materials & textbooks
- living condition is very different between rural and urban
- management is a major problem: primary ed(3); sec. ed(10); higher ed(11); non-formal ed(2)

3.1 Rank in terms of priority the kind of intervention in the primary education sector which you would undertake: (9 choices)

	Total	Gov't	Non-Gov't	LDC-S	LDC-G	SD	N
1. teacher training	2.9	3.7	2.5	3.3	2.9	1.7	44
2. textbooks & materials production	2.9	2.7	3.1	3.0	2.9	1.6	44
3. other	3	5	2.2	4.0	2.6	3.2	7
4. educational planning & analysis	3.2	2.5	3.4	3.1	3.4	2.3	40
5. school health	6.1	6.3	6.1	6.4	5.7	2.2	36

Other: - the need to work for economic reasons
- systems building
- instructional system design
- textbooks and materials distribution
- population policy dialogue
- school nutrition (supplemental meals)
- Distance education
- bilingual education

3.2 Rank Priority Intervention: Secondary Education: (9 choices)

	Total	Gov't	Non-Gov't	LDC-S	LDC-G	SD	N
1. other	2.4	2.0	2.4	4.0	1.3	2.1	5
2. educational planning & analysis	2.5	1.8	2.5	2.9	2.1	1.8	28
3. textbooks and materials production	2.8	2.7	2.8	2.6	2.9	1.5	25

	Average Rating				Standard	
	Total	Gov't	Non-Gov't	LDC-S	LDC-G	Deviation	N
4. teacher training	2.8	2.5	3.1	2.9	2.8	1.4	31
5. school health	7.2	5.8	7.1	7.2	6.2	2.3	20

3.3 Rank Priority intervention: higher education: (9 choices)

	Total	Gov't	Non-Gov't	LDC-S	LDC-G	Std Dev	N
1. educational planning & analysis	2.2	2.0	2.2	2.3	2.0	1.4	25
2. textbooks & materials production	3.3	3.3	3.3	2.3	2.0	1.7	18
3. other	3.3	--	3.3	4.5	1.0	2.5	3
4. teacher training	3.4	3.0	3.7	2.6	4.3	2.4	21
5. curriculum design	3.6	4.2	3.6	3.4	3.9	2.0	21
6. school health	7.0	6.0	7.3	7.1	6.8	2.1	14

3.4 Rank Priority Intervention: Non-Formal education: (9 choices)

	Total	Gov't	Non-Gov't	LDC-S	LDC-G	Std Dev	N
1. educational planning & analysis	2.8	2.7	2.9	2.7	3.0	1.4	18
2. teacher training	3	4.2	2.8	3.0	3.0	1.6	20
3. curriculum design	3.1	3.8	3	3.5	2.7	1.9	20
4. school health	6.8	5.7	7.1	7.0	6.5	2.3	13

Other: - lack of technical and administrative support
      - coherent planning; and decision making process

General Comments on 3.1-3.4:

- There is a need for simultaneous efforts
- Look at content of textbooks and materials production so that gender and class biases are reduced, if not eliminated.
- economic planning for employment and development
- equalization of school quality
- construction leisure time for students (boarders)
- management is priority intervention: prim ed (4); sec ed(4); higher ed(8); non-formal ed (28)

	Average Rating	Standard	
	Total Gov't Non-Gov't LDC-S LDC-G	Deviation	N

4.1 Rank the major problems/needs related to facilities planning and construction: (7 choices)

	Total	Gov't	Non-Gov't	LDC-S	LDC-G	SD	N
1. inadequate equipment & materials	2.2	2.4	2.3	2.1	2.3	1.3	49
2. insufficient maintenance	2.8	2.5	3	2.7	3.1	1.3	42
3. lack of classroom space	3.1	3.3	3	3.5	2.6	1.6	43
4. vandalism	5.3	5.0	5.5	5.1	5.7	1.2	32

Other:
- silly insistence in following Western models of school facilities
- schools are too large; more support needed for 2-3 classroom model for grades 1-5; essential to get schools closer to the home/small villages
- inadequate administration system
- inadequate budgetary allocation
- poor management of resources
- no appreciation for equipment and materials
- inadequate equipment - lack of desks and chairs
- noise interference from both outside activities (e.g. temple fairs) and between classes (29)
- high cost construction models preferred by donors
- inadequate desks, chairs, storage facilities

4.2 Rank the following strategies to address problems in facilities planning and construction: (5 choices)

	Total	Gov't	Non-Gov't	LDC-S	LDC-G	SD	N
1. greater community participation in school construction & maintenance	1.8	1.6	2	1.8	1.9	1.0	46
2. funds for purchase of materials and equipment	2.4	3	2.4	2.6	2.3	1.2	45
3. modify school calendar to maximize use of existing facilities	3	2.9	3.1	3.1	2.9	1.2	40
4. greater reliance on private sector	3.5	3.8	3.4	3.8	3.2	1.4	39
5. training of architects	3.7	3.8	3.8	3.3	4.2	1.4	40

Other:
- work on school finance mechanisms (school bonds and other capital funds and construction loans)
- multi-grade teaching

	Average Rating				Standard	
	Total	Gov't	Non-Gov't	LDC-S	LDC-G	Deviation	N

Comment: Eliminate training of architects and facilities planners and funds for purchase of materials and equipment and increase community participation in school <u>design</u>.

5.1 Rank the major problems/needs related to textbooks and materials production: (8 choices)

	Total	Gov't	Non-Gov't	LDC-S	LDC-G	Std. Dev.	N
1. lack of design and production know-how	2.5	1.7	2.6	2.2	2.8	1.4	42
2. other	2.2	2	2.4	2.8	1.0	2.3	9
3. inadequate curriculum	3.1	3.1	3.1	3.8	2.4	2.4	39
4. printing & publishing facilities	3.3	3.6	3.4	3.2	3.5	1.8	39
5. lack of private sector investment	5.0	5.3	4.9	5.3	4.6	1.7	36

Other:
- materials not coordinated with curriculum/teacher training
- shortage of textbook writing specialists by specialization
- cost recovery
- low quality of mss. Rush to get books written, inadequate vetting (29)
- inadequate distribution system
- training and orientation of authors and editors of books and materials

5.2 Rank the strategies to address problems in textbooks and materials production: (6 choices)

	Total	Gov't	Non-Gov't	LDC-S	LDC-G	Std. Dev.	N
1. training in textbook design & production	1.7	1.4	1.8	1.8	1.5	1.0	41
2. greater investment in printing/publishing plant, equipment and paper supplies	2.7	2.3	3	2.7	2.8	1.3	38
3. other	2.7	2	2.9	2.7	3.0	1.7	8
4. greater privatization of textbook/materials design/production function	2.8	2.7	2.7	2.7	2.8	1.4	41
5. shift to non-print media	3.8	3.9	3.9	3.9	3.7	1.4	34

Other:

- train and motivate teachers to write books
- more than problems of production, there are problems of funding --most of the budget goes to salaries.

- compliment with non-print media
- training and appointment of textbook writers by relevant fields of specialization
- change budget procedures: (a) authorize carrying of funds over several fiscal years; (b) escrow maintenance
- reduce size and increase number and frequency of printing
- work on losses in storage and distribution (rodents, mildew, termites)
- include non-text materials
- ensure local acquisition budget
- better management of existing facilities
- better understanding of the choices in selecting appropriate textbook provisioning systems and of how to organize and manage such systems. Use of appropriate models of successful systems.
- cost recovery

Comments: Rather than greater privatization, cooperation between government and private sector

	Total	Gov't	Non-Gov't	LDC-S	LDC-G	Standard Deviation	N

6.1 Ranking of major problems/needs related to educational planning and analysis: (5 choices)

	Total	Gov't	Non-Gov't	LDC-S	LDC-G	Std Dev	N
1. human resource planning	2.0	2.0	2.0	1.9	2.1	1.0	45
2. organizational systems	2.4	1.9	2.4	2.3	2.5	1.1	44
3. other	2.5	3.0	2.4	3.0	1.7	1.7	8
4. management information systems	2.6	2.4	2.7	2.4	2.8	1.3	46
5. financial planning	2.7	3.3	2.6	3.0	2.3	1.1	45

Other:
- data -- basic census vital data and school census inventories
- manpower
- political forces prevail
- shortage of specialist planners
- integrate into area-oriented development planning
- training of planners
- school mapping
- operational planning for cost-effective policy implementation
- formulation of coherent, internally consistent set of education policies

6.2 Ranking of strategies to address problems in educational planning and analysis: (4 choices)

	Total	Gov't	Non-Gov't	LDC-S	LDC-G	Std Dev	N
1. planning & analytical skills training	1.4	1.4	1.5	1.4	1.5	0.7	49
2. decentralization of planning	2.1	2.2	2.1	2.2	2.0	1.0	44

	Average Rating				Standard	
	Total	Gov't	Non-Gov't	LDC-S	LDC-G	Deviation	N

3. other	2.1	2	2.4	2.4	1.7	1.4	8
4. greater investment in data processing facilities	2.5	2.3	2.5	2.6	2.4	0.6	43

Other:
- collect and compare data -- make sure data is collected/assigned at same level as decisions are made.
- policy analysis training
- input from target student population
- institutionalizing planning and policy analysis
- training in resource management
- training in policy analysis and formulation
- national and local objectives and goals for education and training
- exposing some academics who make a lot of noises without thinking ideas through (29)

7.1 Ranking of the major problems/needs related to curriculum design in primary education: (6 choices)

1. too oriented to rote learning	2.2	2.5	2.1	2.8	1.7	1.3	40
2. not geared to practical life needs	2.4	2.5	2.6	2.1	2.7	1.2	35
3. too geared to examination system	2.9	2.7	3	2.5	3.3	1.4	34
4. not geared to student ability	3.0	2.4	3.1	2.8	3.1	1.4	39
5. inappropriate materials	3.4	2.9	3.7	3.5	3.3	1.5	35

Other: outdated, rigid
- too many subjects being examined
- curriculum does not prepare a student adequately for progression to more higher level
- curriculum not structured in terms of priority and sequentially-ordered learning objectives, varied learning strategies with supporting educational media and materials for students and teachers, and measures of learning
- demonstration schools

Comment: Often devised in urban settings and subject to latest imported trends, with too little regard to actual classroom situations outside urban centers.

7.2 Ranking of needs related to curriculum design in secondary education: (6 choices)

1. not geared to practical life needs	2.2	3	2.2	2.1	2.3	1.1	25
2. too geared to examination system	2.2	2	2.3	1.7	2.8	1.5	26

	Average Rating				Standard	
	Total	Gov't	Non-Gov't	LDC-S	LDC-G	Deviation	N
3. other	2.6	2.5	2.7	3.0	2.0	1.5	5
4. too oriented to rote learning	3.1	2.3	3.2	4.0	2.0	1.7	25
5. not geared to student ability	3.2	2.0	3.6	3.3	3.2	1.1	25
6. inappropriate materials	3.3	3.0	3.4	3.2	3.3	1.5	25

Other: Keep curriculum flexible and responsive to change. Allow for creative interpretation in textbook materials, variety and choice.

7.3 Ranking of needs related to curriculum design in higher education: (6 choices)

1. too geared to examination system	2.2	2.5	2.2	2.0	2.4	1.1	22
2. not geared to practical life needs	2.3	2.5	2.4	2.2	2.5	1.3	23
3. too oriented to rote learning	2.9	1	3	3.2	2.5	1.5	22
4. other	1.5	2	1	2.0	1.3	0.6	4
5. inappropriate materials	3.2	3.0	3.3	3.6	2.8	1.3	23
6. not geared to student ability	3.3	3.0	3.4	2.7	3.9	1.5	21

7.4. Ranking of needs related to curriculum design in non-formal education: (6 choices)

1. not geared to practical needs	2.2	1	2.5	2.4	2.1	1.1	17
2. not geared to student abilities	2.6	2	2.6	2.3	2.9	1.4	18
3. inappropriate materials	2.8	1.7	3.1	2.7	3.0	1.3	19
4. other	1.5	2	1	2.0	1.0	0.7	2
5. too oriented to rote learning	3.2	3.0	3.2	3.4	2.9	1.4	16

Other :
- curriculum is overloaded with more objectives than resources permit.
- not geared to labor market needs
- modified to address country languages and customs
- none of the above applies to non-formal education

Comment on 7.1-7.4:

- failure in curriculum implementation according to basic principles of curriculum

	Average Rating				Standard	
	Total	Gov't	Non-Gov't	LDC-S	LDC-G	Deviation	N

7.5 Ranking of strategies to address problems in curriculum design in primary education: (5 choices)

	Total	Gov't	Non-Gov't	LDC-S	LDC-G	SD	N
1. train teachers to make better use	1.9	1.7	2.1	1.9	2.1	0.9	42
2. develop improved materials	2	1.8	2.1	2.1	1.9	1.0	42
3. training to upgrade design skills	2.7	2.2	2.8	2.7	2.7	1.0	37
4. tie to student assessment	2.7	3.1	2.6	2.7	2.8	1.1	36

Other:
-design an instructional system
-reduce range of examinable subjects

7.6 Ranking of strategies to address problems in curriculum design in secondary education: (5 choices)

	Total	Gov't	Non-Gov't	LDC-S	LDC-G	SD	N
1. develop improved materials	1.9	2	1.9	2.1	1.8	0.9	31
2. train teachers to make better use	2.2	1.3	2.5	2.2	2.1	1.1	31
3. tie to student assessment	2.5	3.7	2.2	2.4	2.5	1.2	25
4. training to upgrade design	3.0	2.8	3.0	2.9	3.0	1.2	25

7.7 Ranking of strategies to address problems in curriculum design in higher education: (5 choices)

	Total	Gov't	Non-Gov't	LDC-S	LDC-G	SD	N
1. develop improved materials	2.0	1.8	2.1	1.9	2.0	0.9	25
2. train teachers to make better use	2.1	1.5	2.4	2.2	2.1	1.1	23
3. tie to student assessment	2.6	3.5	2.6	2.9	2.3	1.2	21
4. upgrade design skills	2.8	3.0	2.8	2.9	2.6	1.3	23

7.8 Ranking of strategies to address problems in curriculum design in non-formal education: (5 choices)

	Total	Gov't	Non-Gov't	LDC-S	LDC-G	SD	N
1. develop improved materials	1.8	2	1.9	1.8	1.9	0.8	18
2. train teachers to make better use	2.3	2.5	2.3	2.4	2.1	1.0	19
3. tie to student assessment	2.5	1	2.6	2.4	2.6	1.3	16
4. other	2.7	3	2.5	2.7	---	1.5	3
5. upgrade design skills	3.1	3.0	3.1	3.5	2.9	1.3	16

Other: simplify, reduce content to essentials and to time/resources available

Comment: Curriculum is too geared to examination system: in non-formal schools students study for certificate and use the same curriculum as in normal school

Comment: 7.5-7.8

- fostering proper understanding of objectives of curriculum among agencies and educators, administrators concerned
- training administrators for the implementation of curriculum
- allow teachers, former students to help design curriculum

8.1 Ranking of the major problems/needs related to teachers: (8 choices)

1. salaries and incentives	2.4	2.3	2.6	2.2	2.3	1.7	47
2. selection and recruitment	3.1	2.8	3.2	2.8	3.7	1.9	39
3. pre-service training	3.2	3.6	3.2	3.2	3.3	1.7	44
4. higher percent of budget spent on teachers	5.3	4.6	5.7	5.6	4.9	2.2	35

Other:
- lack of commitment
- professional administrators to provide leadership
- assignment of teachers to most relevant areas
- important but real problem is insufficient MOE budget all around
- terrible work conditions discourage most good teachers. Problem is how to retain/motivate - teachers, not how to train/recruit.
- teachers leaving profession in big numbers
- management support for teachers is poor
- pre-service training geared practically to teaching conditions

8.2 Ranking of the strategies to address problems related to teachers: (9 choices)

1. strengthening of finance & incentives support	2.8	3	2.9	2.8	2.8	1.9	46
2. improved in-service training	3.5	3.3	3.7	3.6	3.5	2.0	49
3. improved pre-service training	3.7	3.7	3.9	3.8	3.7	2.1	46
4. other	2.3	--	3	1.0	3.0	1.5	3
5. give teachers more autonomy	5.4	6.3	5.2	5.6	5.1	2.1	35
5. reduce dependence through alternative delivery	6.0	5.5	6.2	6.4	5.6	2.4	37

Other:
- motivation/commitment of local teachers
- decentralization for community control

	Average Rating					Standard	
	Total	Gov't	Non-Gov't	LDC-S	LDC-G	Deviation	N

- make textbooks and teacher editions tools for instructing both teachers and pupils
- greater administrative leadership

8.3 Ranking of techniques for improving instruction: (5 choices)

	Total	Gov't	Non-Gov't	LDC-S	LDC-G	SD	N
1. diagnostic/prescriptive instruction	1.9	2.1	1.9	1.9	1.9	1.0	41
2. mastery learning	2.3	1.6	2.5	2.5	2.1	1.2	43
3. other	2.4	1.7	2.9	2.5	2.4	1.9	11
4. individualized instruction	2.5	3.6	2.2	2.4	2.6	1.1	38
5. peer tutoring	3.6	3.6	2.9	3.1	2.7	1.0	42

Other:
- emphasis on time-on-task use of master teachers
- let teachers teach
- distance teaching with media support
- practical learning
- better teacher:pupil ratio
- better facilities and materials
- don't reject rote learning entirely
- self-instruction and self-correcting materials
- extra time tutoring in difficult subject areas
- Distance learning/teaching
- structure motivation, appropriateness clear objectives and a program that can be mastered by the average teacher/pupil in the time available!
- group instruction (semi individualized)

Comment: mastery learning (semi programmed text books)
- not sure any of these are appropriate taken in isolation

9.1 Ranking of the major problems related to testing and evaluation: (5 choices)

	Total	Gov't	Non-Gov't	LDC-S	LDC-G	SD	N
1. lack of assessment procedures to diagnose	1.8	1.8	1.8	1.6	2.0	0.9	46
2. other	1.9	1	2	1.8	2.0	1.7	10
3. lack of accountability of student performance	2.6	2.2	2.7	2.4	2.9	1.2	40
4. lack of appropriate grade and subject matter exams	2.7	1.9	3	3.0	2.3	1.2	44
5. inability to compare student performance across schools	3.6	3.6	2.9	3.1	2.9	1.0	42

Other:
- tests are not secure, not reliably normed, not stable across cultures and teachers have no ability to respond to any identified problems
- lack of standard control in evaluation
- lack of student interest
- lack of skills of testing and evaluation
- lack of parents/teacher dialogue on students' performance
- effects of socio economic and community variables including mother language
- assessment procedures are based on European values
- administration/feedback
- overemphasis on certification thru exams
- testing is unrelated to societal needs

Feedback: I don't believe in standardized testing
-heavy emphasis on tests can be counterproductive to learning

9.2 Ranking of strategies to address problems related to testing and evaluation: (5 choices)

	Total	Gov't	Non-Gov't	LDC-S	LDC-G	Standard Deviation	N
1. increase teacher assessment skills	2.0	2	2.1	1.9	2.3	1.2	41
2. introduce grade-level ref'nce tests	2.6	2.7	2.7	2.8	2.4	1.4	43
3. develop standardized achievement tests	2.9	2.2	2.9	2.8	2.9	1.4	37
4. training to increase national capacity in tests and measurement	3.4	3.4	3.4	3.5	3.2	1.2	43

Other: % of repeaters in first grade (over 50% now on average!!!)

10.1 Ranking of major problems related to the use of educational technologies: (7 choices)

	Total	Gov't	Non-Gov't	LDC-S	LDC-G	Standard Deviation	N
1. lack of knowledge about use of specific technologies	2.8	2.1	3.0	2.8	2.8	1.5	44
2. other	2.8	5.5	1.7	5.0	1.8	2.4	6
3. lack of technical know-how	2.9	3.2	2.8	2.7	3.1	1.3	42
3. high capital costs	3.0	2.6	3.1	3.0	3.0	2.0	40
4. technology perceived as a threat	4.1	4.2	4.3	4.6	3.5	2.0	39

Other: - organizational weakness, difficulty sustaining anything not keyed to conventional budgets and staffing. System already overloaded; unless technology makes something easier to do, not just done better, it will not be adopted readily or sustained.
- lack of power and isolation
- budget does not accommodate
- fashions come and go
- failure to develop social consensus among key actors (eg; teachers, headmasters, education leaders) for using new education technologies
- failure to establish cost-effectiveness relative to other learning inputs
- social marketing re: cost-effectiveness where this can be established
- strengthening of consensus among key constituencies

Comment: lack of technical know-how (30% of teachers have not finished high school)

Feedback: Depends on what technologies we are talking about. I'm in favor of home-made visual aids, not imported goods.
- Which technologies, for what reason?
- What kind of technology? In most countries (Third World), I am familiar with, good textbooks, some library resources (maps, posters, charts) and modest lab and workshop equipment would be a marked improvement. !

10.2 Ranking of ways to address problems related to the use of educational technologies: (6 choices)

	Total	Gov't	Non-Gov't	LDC-S	LDC-G	Standard Deviation	N
1. training to increase technical know-how	2.1	2	2.1	1.9	2.4	0.8	42
2. other	2.2	1	3.5	1.0	2.7	2.5	4
3. small pilot projects to demonstrate feasibility	2.4	2.2	2.6	2.6	2.2	1.4	44
4. training to increase national awareness of potential of various technology	2.5	2.2	2.6	2.5	2.6	1.3	42
5. gov't incentives to entrepreneurs	4.0	4.9	4.0	4.0	4.0	1.2	36

Feedback: training to increase technical know-how in educational technology using local resources and creativity.
Other: - provide incentive to teacher in form of compensation or reduced burden
- design appropriate technology (for example "Escuela Nueva" in Colombia)
- Development of appropriate technologies

	Average Rating					Standard	
	Total	Gov't	Non-Gov't	LDC-S	LDC-G	Deviation	N

10.3 Ranking of technologies for impact on teaching and learning: (8 choices)

	Total	Gov't	Non-Gov't	LDC-S	LDC-G	Std Dev	N
1. microcomputers	3.2	2.6	3.3	3.4	2.9	2.0	39
2. radio	3.2	2.8	3.5	3.7	2.7	2.4	46
3. video cassette recorders	3.5	3.0	3.7	3.5	3.6	1.7	42
4. television	3.6	4.7	3.3	3.9	3.1	1.8	39
5. satellite communications	4.9	5.1	4.8	5.2	4.5	2.2	35

Other:
- domestically designed and prepared low-cost visual aids; e.g. charts, models, etc.
- Educational package "Escuela Nueva"
- distance teaching
- textbooks, teacher's editions, supplemental materials.
- radio in Africa; microcomputers at university level; satellite communications in Asia
- It depends on the level of education and whether public/private offerings.
- 35 mm slide projector still very important

Feedback: Too broad a question -- teaching/learning what?
- depends on region

11.1 Ranking of the major problems/needs related to school health: (5 choices)

	Total	Gov't	Non-Gov't	LDC-S	LDC-G	Std Dev	N
1. lack of data on extent of school health problems and their effect on learning	1.9	1.1	2.1	2.0	1.7	1.1	42
2. insufficient school health facilities	2.0	2.6	1.9	2.2	1.8	0.9	39
3. inappropriate school feeding programs and policies	2.8	2.9	2.9	3.0	2.5	1.0	39
4. lack of school health standards	2.8	2.7	2.8	2.6	3.2	1.1	35

Other:
- inadequate inoculations; overcrowding; poor nutrition in the home; endemic fevers and parasites.
- national ego to refuse admission of problems
- no cooperation between education and health officials
- inadequate water and sanitation services.

	Average Rating					Standard	
	Total	Gov't	Non-Gov't	LDC-S	LDC-G	Deviation	N

11.2 Ranking of ways to address problems related to school health: (6 choices)

	Total	Gov't	Non-Gov't	LDC-S	LDC-G	SD	N
1. strengthening of school health facilities	2.4	2.9	2.3	2.6	2.0	1.3	39
2. epidemiological research into school health problems	2.7	1.7	2.9	3.0	2.4	1.7	43
3. enactment of national school health standards	2.8	3.3	2.7	3.0	2.6	1.1	34
4. strengthen school feeding policy & programs	3.1	3.3	3.1	3.3	28	1.5	38

Other: - immunization campaign
 - potable water in the school
 - diagnosis of vision/hearing problems
 - parasite prophylactics and curative/purgative
 - larger classrooms
 - increase awareness in communities

12. Ranking of format in which technical assistance and training in education is most useful: (6 choices)

	Total	Gov't	Non-Gov't	LDC-S	LDC-G	SD	N
1. short-term, in-country training	2.8	2.2	3.0	2.8	2.9	1.7	46
2. technical prob-solving & analysis	2.8	3.9	2.6	3.4	2.4	1.6	41
3. project design and evaluation	2.9	3.5	2.7	3.1	2.7	1.4	42
4. short-term overseas training	3.0	3.2	2.4	2.9	3.2	1.4	42
5. policy dialogue	3.6	3.0	3.8	3.9	3.6	1.8	40
4. long-term overseas training	3.9	3.1	4.2	3.2	4.3	1.9	40

Other: - developing appropriate institutions in Third World settings
 - training plus collaborative problem solving
 - start a long-term project and make use of local expertise
 - long-term in-service training

Comment:
 - long-term, overseas training <u>for selected educators</u>.
 - these are problem specific
 - use of the above depends on the kind of technical assistance

	Average Rating	Standard	

	Total	Gov't	Non-Gov't	LDC-S	LDC-G	Standard Deviation	N

13. Ranking of problems related to the delivery of technical assistance in education: (6 choices)

	Total	Gov't	Non-Gov't	LDC-S	LDC-G	Std Dev	N
1. lack of understanding of local context	2.1	2.6	2.0	2.1	2.2	1.0	43
2. lack of long-term linkages between providers and receivers	2.7	2	2.9	2.7	2.8	1.3	45
3. assumes western model of development	2.8	3.6	2.6	3.0	2.7	1.7	38
4. other	1.7	1	2	1.0	2.0	1.2	3
5. time horizon of intervention is too short	3.1	2.5	2.4	3.5	2.6	1.4	46

Other:
- unrealistic expectations on all sides of how much can be accomplished how fast
- excessive concern with finding a new solution for each context
- lack of adequate local counterparts in terms of intellectual quality, commitment and authority (in Shakespearean sense of King Lear)
- lack of promotion local people to solve their own problems
- Assistance is piece-meal, directed at only part of th e problem; few assistance projects result in the creation of permanent institutions, carrying on the work of the project with trained staff and secure financing.
- misplaced emphasis on changes in technology rather than changes in administrative systems, organization or political-economic basis for financing and policy decisions.
- technological activities hands-on, problem solving

Comments:
- Yes, everyone of those, are equally important. Therefore, these issues must be avoided! However, when UNDP gives assistance for the establishment of IPST, most of these problems were eliminated, and the project is quite successful.

Most successful use of technical assistance in an education project in a developing country:

— The provision of free textbooks for all children in primary schools in Mexico
— At primary level, textbook projects such as World Bank financed project in the Philippines
— For higher education, long-term overseas training and in-country long-term technical support
— Demonstration projects for teacher training
— Low-cost textbook production in Jamaica
— Financial planning model in Zimbabwe
— School mapping in Egypt
— Human resources training that can self-perpetuate
— Giving money to a good NGO and letting it develop with the community whatever they think is appropriate
— Financing the project
— Advisory and expertise support
— In-service training, workshop in specific field
— To develop domestic capability in providing effective staff development programs and producing teaching aids and materials
— In Thailand, the project for the Improvement of Secondary English Teaching in co-operation with the British government has set up a number of ERICs (English Resources and Instruction Centers) to serve other schools nearby. The project also includes overseas in-service training to make the centers more effective
— The use of radio, television-audio cassette recorders and video cassette recorders in programs of distance education in Colombia
— Overseas training and exposure for teachers and education administrators has been the most successful use of technical assistance for most D/Cs
— Training, especially short-term training, and collaborative projects that develop research capacity
— The assistance to set up the Maritime Institute of Education and the loan for the construction of buildings and provision of equipment for the secondary schools in Mauritius
— Comprehensive development project for schools in a particular local area

- Some of the work done on World Bank university development projects in Indonesia
- The development of written curriculum and introduction to use of visual aids
- SIDA/NORAD purchase of books and desks for Zambian secondary schools in 1984-86; general upgrading of physical facilities and the organization of maintenance support staff
- Radio education/textbook production assistance/teacher training
- Training of personnel; provision of learning material (Pakistan)
- Those with greatest dialogue and planning based on local content
- At primary level, textbook projects such as World Bank financed project in Philippines
- Training of 60 Ecuadorian instructors by Lab Volt during summer of 1986
- To show that repetition was much higher than the levels filled by principal in statistical forms (50% instead of 15 to 20%) in first grade
- ILO Turin Training Center
- Review of curriculum and facilities of teacher/instructor skills, upgrading of curriculum and teacher/instructor upgrading
- Short-term consultants looking at situation with fresh eyes and making recommendations. In certain areas expatriate experts guiding personnel through difficult phases of development to create awareness of desirable standards
- El Salvador ITV Project, Liberian Rural Communications System
- Setting up an MIS for data collection and improved administration will also lead to improved policy making
- Establishment of distance teaching system for secondary and higher education in Kenya
- Peace Corps and the AFS exchange student programs
- Promotion of teaching science project in Thailand beginning from Pilot Project through to the establishment of IPST. The work has had a great deal of influence on this region
- Helping in the use of model development on research methodology
- Assessing cost-effectiveness of policy options; assistance in developing/producing/disseminating instructional material

- The setting up of teacher training facilities
- TA useful if he/she can persuade developing countries to take a chance on adopting pro-change of proven value (eg educational reform)
- Assessment of problems related to education based on data pertaining to school performance
- Infra-structure
- How to efficiently grow and preserve local foods
- Capacity building, especially in human capital, not facilities
- Money for facilities construction, the need is clear and there are no problems of fit or conflict with existing structures or ways of doing things. Other things are needed but they are more likely to run up against obstacles. The technical people are scarcely sensitive to fits and sensitivity to culture is rare.
- Radio for teaching basic skills and competency-based instruction in vocational skills

Kind of training and/or technical assistance most beneficial to developing countries:

- Primary/Secondary: management and planning; Universities: discipline-specific and management
- Development-oriented education for increasing productivity (internal and external) on all levels
- Explicit training in role functions that help build systems. For teachers, focused training in methods for using explicit support materials that have been tested and clearly produce the learning results desired
- Policy-analysis skills, research methods, information gathering and analysis
- Technical know-how in local context
- Training of trainers to enhance learning process. Development of training programs related to the country's needs
- Technical know-how and training to maintain optimal performance of infrastructure provided and planning requirements thereof
- Advice with regard to policy change, help with administration of large-scale projects
- Short-term consultants to assess problems and make recommendations. Professional services in areas in which local

expertise is available, e.g. broadcasting engineering if the country is building new facilities
- Technology and basic sciences
- The project that would suit immediate interests and needs of people, i.e., craft design and technology education is seen as beneficial. Through it, people can solve everyday problems and earn a living
- Workshop training
- Development of distance teaching, materials for use on national and regional basis of secondary, higher and non-formal education
- Teacher training. Social marketing to improve status of teachers. Finding creative ways to increase teachers' salaries
- A combination of academic and practical education
- Assistance and training in educational policy formulation, operational education, plan development and implementation, instructional system design
- Provision of textbooks (primary and secondary) for students and instructional guides for teachers would be single most beneficial contribution
- Review of curriculum and facilities of teacher/instructor skills, upgrading of curriculum and teacher/instructor upgrading bearing in mind that assessments and upgrading training must be in keeping with local customs, beliefs, government restrictions, budgets and plans for economic development
- Design and use of management information systems
- Long-term technical training of instructors on practical equipment
- Developing educational research capacity, especially in ministries of education. Capacity in fields such as educational finance and testing and measurement and curriculum evaluation
- Building institutions that will effectively transfer experience and technical know-how in the total process of developing educational materials provisioning systems, and at the same time train practitioners and offer technical assistance in a Third World setting
- Long-term linkages based strictly on understanding of local context
- Teacher training (pre and in-service)

- Training of planners and managers; training of teacher educators (Pakistan)
- Training to encourage MOE's to think flexibly and creatively about alternatives to formal education on a national level
- Management systems, policy analysis in central offices
- Curriculum development, written materials for teaching methods and use of many aids in presentation of material
- Training in the management and planning of education and technical assistance for curriculum development and evaluation in Mauritius
- Teacher training overseas; refresher courses in-country; teacher exchange schemes between D/C's and Developed Countries
- Training to increase national awareness of potential of various technologies and to increase technical know-how in educational technology
- Training in education system planning with emphasis on resources mobilization and utilization in connection with severe resource constraints
- Develop a corps of educators and community leaders for the active pilot areas that could initiate a spreading effect to neighboring communities—on a self-help basis
- An appropriate package comprising good services, fellowships for both in-country and overseas training of key persons and essential equipment/material to achieve effective transfer of technology or address major issues
- On-site, continuous advice/support by a knowledgeable yet modest educator
- Provision of textbooks and teacher training for elementary schools
- Long term, in-country technical support
- Long-term technical in-country assistance in stable institutions in the country as well as long term in-country or overseas training has proven successful
- Planning, policy formulation, curriculum development, instructional technology, efficiency management
- Facilities construction, equipment, teacher training, financial assistance, etc.
- Too general a question—start with the basics of system management and logistics and work up and out to optional choices and refinements

- Convincing governments to pay more attention to education, and to increased investment in education, but do so efficiently
- Modern modes and methods of teaching; analyzing the educational system; diagnosis supervision; clinical supervision
- Training in educational planning and management will be most beneficial to a developing country. Another area of current interest is specific training in science and technology that could be applied to teaching-learning situation in a rural set-up

Training Questionnaire
Summary of Results

	Average Total	N	Stnd Dev	Non-Gov't	Gov't	LDC-S	LDC-G
1. Rank primary goals for training and development (12 options)							
1. employment generation	2.3	47	1.9	2.2	2.4	2.1	2.4
2. training primarily for economic development	2.5	46	1.9	2.6	2.4	2.5	2.4
3. increased quality of training	2.7	48	1.3	2.8	2.9	2.6	2.7
4. shift of public resources from academic education to vocational training	4.6	37	2.6	4.9	4.5	4.9	4.2
5. increased opportunities for women	5.6	40	2.6	6.3	5.5	5.9	5.5
6. requirement of teacher certification exams	6.6	34	2.3	6.7	6.4	6.1	7.0
7. national certification program established for various levels of workers	6.8	37	6.3	6.0	9.2	7.6	6.0
8. industry to provide teacher training	6.9	37	3.2	7.8	4.9	5.7	7.8
9. substantial increases in teacher salaries	7.4	35	3.4	7.2	8.0	8.3	6.9
10. national competency exams required for all students	7.4	36	2.7	7.6	6.9	6.9	7.7
11. training health workers considered a good investment	7.6	32	3.0	7.3	8.5	7.4	7.4

Other
- Residential training centers (especially for juvenile delinquents and disadvantaged youngsters)
- Increased quantity of training
- Export oriented, to create foreign capital
- Upgrade existing facilities in vocational training
- Management of education-school systems
- Career guidance and work transition help
- Improve the human condition
- training for self-employment/income-generation
- Rural development and micro-enterprise development
- improved equipment for training
- provide facilities and equipment for training purposes
- Training for rural communities; training for self employment and income generation in rural areas

	Average Total	N	Stnd Dev	Non-Gov't	Gov't	LDC-S	LDC-G

2. Rank basis for planning, analyis and assessment of the training system (10 options)

1. satisfaction of manpower requirements	2.5	46	1.7	2.7	2.5	2.2	2.8
2. concentration on training programs that are justified by labor market information	2.8	46	1.7	2.6	3.6	3.2	2.3
3. provision of skills for job creation and entrepreneurial purposes	3.1	45	1.7	3.2	3.1	2.9	3.3
4. highly centralized training, policy and funding	6.3	34	3.0	6.5	5.8	5.6	6.8

Other:
- Local employer input into planning & assessment
- use cluster training rather than job specific

3. Rank the following cost and constraint trends: (12 options)

1. inadequate supply of trained vocational teachers	2.8	44	1.6	2.8	3.3	2.6	2.8
2. cost as a major factor limiting program development	2.8	45	2.0	3.1	2.3	3.1	2.6
3. the lack of financial resources	2.9	46	2.1	3.1	2.4	2.2	3.4
4. institutional training facilities not fully utilized	8.1	33	2.4	7.9	8.6	8.5	7.8

Other:
- Lack of proper public policy
- Low salary of teachers that results to poor motivation
- Family perception of "Voc Ed"
- Political
- Technical education viewed by families as second class. It is better to have a Ph.D. and be unemployed.

	Average Total	N	Stnd Dev	Non-Gov't	Averages Gov't	LDC-S	LDC-G

Comments:
- PVO term not known
- What is a PVO?
- Inadequate planning/management of training function

4. Rank the following uses of modern equipment and pedagogy: (10 options)

1. educational technology generally	1.8	41	1.2	1.9	1.7	1.9	1.8
2. educational technology to off-set the lack of trained teachers	3.1	39	1.7	3.2	2.5	2.8	3.2
3. computers a major instructional tool	4.0	42	2.2	4.1	3.8	3.8	4.4
4. minicomputers to deliver up to half or more of the training	6.6	34	2.4	6.5	6.9	7.0	6.2

Other
- This is not clear and not relevant to the Caribbean
- Appropriate technology, not just high tech
- Video assisted (video based)
- Basics are the most needed, <u>not</u> modern equipment
- Most training centers of the govt agency are still using obsolete equipment
- Distance learning with appropriate technology
- use of mobile technology

5. Rank training needs for industrial development in the following sectors: (7 options)

1. small and medium size enterprises	2.3	45	1.2	2.3	2.5	2.1	2.4
2. small enterprises	2.7	46	1.8	2.9	2.5	2.1	2.4
3. employments requiring high level training	3.1	46	1.8	3.0	3.3	3.3	2.8
4. rural areas	3.4	44	1.8	3.6	2.8	2.8	3.7
5. urban	3.7	45	1.4	3.7	3.7	3.4	3.8
5. large enterprises	4.2	42	1.7	4.4	3.7	3.6	4.5

Other:
- Nonformal sector
- Vocational instructors
- concentrate on service occupations

	Average Total	N	Stnd Dev	Non-Gov't	Averages Gov't	LDC-S	LDC-G

6. Rank in terms of accuracy, statements of agriculture and rural needs: (4 options)

1. greater emphasis on training for rural development	1.3	46	0.6	1.4	1.2	1.3	1.4
2. training focus on agriculture sector	1.9	41	0.6	2.0	1.9	1.7	2.0
3. training in the agricultural sector more important than training for industrial sector	2.8	40	0.7	2.8	2.7	2.7	2.8

Other:
- Depends on individual countries
- Training on non-form sector
- Agro-industrial and intermediate industries
- Inadequate funding & management on rural training programs
- training for entrepreneurship
- Availability of materials from specific areas

7. Rank in order of importance/emphasis directed toward training for the: (2 options)

1. formal sector	1.5	46	0.5	1.5	1.5	1.5	1.5
2. informal sector	1.5	45	0.5	1.5	1.5	1.5	1.5

Comments:
- Absolutely depends upon local employment conditions
- Both are important but the formal sector is more able to provide training; the informal sector needs more help.

8. Rank in terms of priority the following policy options: (15 options)

1. most training programs to combine training with work experience	2.3	49	2.1	2.3	3.0	2.4	2.2
2. formal training to provide specific skill training just prior to job entry	4.2	40	3.4	4.2	4.3	3.7	4.4

	Average Total	N	Stnd Dev	Non-Gov't	Averages Gov't	LDC-S	LDC-G
3. retraining and upgrading to be more important than initial skill development	5.0	37	3.3	5.3	4.9	4.6	5.3
4. most training to take place within industry	5.7	37	4.0	5.8	5.5	5.7	5.6
5. responsibility of vocational training shifted to ministries of labor	9.9	32	4.4	10.5	8.2	8.5	10.4

Other: - Ministries of Labor and Ministries of Education to form a centralized unit for training

9. Technical assistance for training and development will require: (4 options)

	Average Total	N	Stnd Dev	Non-Gov't	Averages Gov't	LDC-S	LDC-G
1. technical cooperation to analyze retraining needs	1.6	47	0.6	1.6	1.8	1.8	1.5
2. a greater reliance on UN agencies to analyze, design and assist in implementing training	2.2	41	0.9	2.3	2.2	2.2	2.2
3. less use of external experts; national experts should provide most of the support services needed for program development	2.2	41	1.0	2.3	1.8	1.7	2.6

Other:
- International coopertion with internal and external experts working together through a multitude of network organisations
- A total effort: UNDP, World Bank, Asian Bank, in country support, etc.
- UN should provide year-end evaluation of traiing equipment for updating training capability
- Local capability to determine training needs to be upgraded
- Again, depends upon local needs
- Financial assistance
- Outside experts are required to help in administration. Planning, implementation but major responsibility spent rest with in-country experts.
- Needs will dictate next step
- T.A. at the training policy/planning level

	Average Total	N	Stnd Dev	Non-Gov't	Averages Gov't	LDC-S	LDC-G

10. Rank the needs for technical cooperation in respect to: (5 options)

1. facilitating policy for training	2.2	47	1.1	2.3	1.9	2.2	2.1
2. evaluation of training policies, implementation and outcomes	2.4	48	1.1	2.5	2.4	2.3	2.4
3. establishing data bases related to training needs and outputs	2.5	45	1.3	2.7	2.4	1.9	3.0

Other:
Analysing Training needs
Occupational standards development & certification
Work value development

13. Rank format where technical assistance and training in education is most useful: (6 options)

1. short-term, in-country training	2.8	46	1.7	2.9	2.3	2.6	2.9
2. technical problem solving and analysis	2.9	41	1.6	2.8	3.9	3.1	2.6
3. project design and evaluation	2.9	42	1.4	2.8	3.5	2.7	3.0
4. short-term overseas training	3.0	45	1.4	3.2	2.4	2.7	3.2
5. policy dialogue	3.6	40	1.9	3.8	3.0	3.8	3.4
6. long-term overseas training	3.9	40	1.9	4.2	3.1	3.5	4.2

Comment:
- This really depends on the type of program
- The best is a combination of short-term in-country followed by short-term overseas followed by long-term in-service, in-country follow-up training.
- These can't be ranked unless one knows the specific purpose of the activity. They all are important and of top priority depending on the activity.
- What about long-term, in-country training?
- This may vary with the situation. In some cases there is no facility, equipment or instructional material available. If a different language is encountered, it compounds the problem of indigenous instruction. Bringing trainers or trainees to a developed country also poses limitations to persons.

	Average Total	N	Stnd Dev	Non-Gov't	Gov't	LDC-S	LDC-G

14. Rank problems related to delivery of technical assistance: (6 options)

1. lack of long-term linkages between providers and receiver	2.2	45	1.2	2.2	2.7	1.8	2.4
2. lack of understanding of local context	2.4	45	1.2	2.5	1.8	2.1	2.5
3. assistance is provided without transferring technical know-how	2.9	42	1.4	3.0	2.5	2.7	3.0
4. time horizon of intervention is too short	2.9	41	1.4	3.0	2.7	2.7	3.1
5. assumes western model of development	3.5	42	1.6	3.5	3.4	3.8	3.3

Other:
- Planning and project finding
- Host country mismanagement of funds to thepoint that less than half of T.A. funds are actually spent on T.A. the rest on "administration", or "something."
- Poor management of training programs
- Lack of counterpart commitment and support
- Pre-service training of those who go abroad
- Technical consultants working side by side with officials of developing countries over a long period of time.
- Establishing institutional sistership with similar institutions to exchange views and visits
- Problems vary on the maintenance of the training equipment. After the launching the project, the equipment has been left unattended either it is still operational for training and or being obsolete. Technical assistance is thorough, but the assessments/evaluation of training equipment is neglected.

11. Please describe what you think has been the most successful use of technical assistance in a training project in a developing country:
— Assistance through a focused approach to analyze jobs, then training needs using the incumbent worker as expert and the industry to validate results
— (1) Preparing instructional materials in local languages, (2) establishing national certification system based on recognized national occupational classification and description
— In-service education for current teachers provided by T.A.s
— When a good team of experts can work co-operatively with nationals on clear policies and goals, helping to implement
— The establishment of the capacity to train trainers and to set national occupational skill standards
— To provide appropriate information and materials according to user's needs, and if possible to assist planning, including finding financial resources
— Training for rural development activities is helpful using systems approach to training
— Training for rural development
— (1) USAID-OAS Regional Non-formal skills training program in E. Caribbean; (2) OCAD Project; (3) Barbados Community College
— Only have my personal experience training extension agents twice in Somalia
— Maintenance is a must for equipment in a developing country. Spare parts, knowledge of how to keep it operational
— Training needs that are realistic in meeting economic development needs
— To assist countries in developing their own institutional capacity; institution building (not brick & mortar) to allow countries to develop their own training.
— Policy development/data base development
— Develop strong counterpart relationships that span over time and that are targeted towards specific problems and goals
— Depends on country and needs
— Training of current management personnel in methods for adapting existing curriculum materials and related instructional methods
— Saudi Arabia — GOTEVOT (General organization for

technical education and vocational training) took a long-term systems approach to their technical assistance needs
— Provide the developing countries good, well-proven resource people to help them determine their needs and direction
— Train the trainer programs in Western Africa
— T.A. on the training implementation level for establishing and maintaining a training quality to meet industrial standards
— T.A. in which close links have been forged between users and suppliers of skills (eg. between training centers and their clients)
— Technical staff development through fellowships on trainers' training basis
— Upgrading manpower capabilities to meet needs of specific industrial sectors
— Providing short-term consultants and creating a pool of qualified administrators to take over the management of the project. Teachers also need to be prepared from the indigenous population
— Technical assistance provided helps the local people to develop their competencies and utilize them in the relevant field
— Participant/counterpart training that is customized to meet the needs of individuals who have to carry out the programs
— Teacher training, facilities development, equipment support, educational policy
— Upgrading the skills of host country counterparts; upgrading the institutional performance
— Technical co-operation to analyze retraining needs
— Assisting team of nationals in the design, evaluation and implementation of training programs. Financial assistance and evaluation of training programs
— Fellowship programs out of the country & in-service training
— Developing the training system and increasing the quality of instructors
— Technology transfer
— Technical assistance is of only short-term value unless it is institutionalized within the agency in country. Technology transfer must be a part of T.A.
— Provide training opportunities to trainers to update their competencies as demanded by industry
— Training in how to analyze needs; training for maintenance of

equipment; time use of employed workers
— Development of technical examinations programme in Malawi by City and Guilds/British Council Support

12. Please describe briefly what kind of training and/or technical assistance could be most beneficial to developing countries in the field of training:
— Policy dialogue; helping efficient institutions and incorporating local industries in training and transfer of appropriate technologies
— Train the in-country trainers, in all aspects of training
— Upgrading the quality of instructors
— Provision of training equipment, exposure to current trends in technology
— Improvement and upgrading of facilities, supply of spare parts and maintenance of equipment
— Areas of agriculture, water and energy
— Skill updating of trainers to levels demanded by industry
— (1) more emphasis on teacher training and methodology; (2) adequate instructional materials; (3) adequate maintenance program (equipment & facilities)
— Retraining model (curriculum design)
— Provide teaching skills taking into account the needs of the country especially vocational training
— Closer linkages between all aspects of T.A. including equipment procurement, curriculum development, training needs
— Organization, curriculum, technical assistance
— Master trainers to be trained to provide training to the field staff
— There is a need for improved planning, technology transfer, and evaluation of new programs being launched
— Evaluation is the weakest link. You can't conduct evaluation if standards are not established
— Development of institutional infrastructure; training of trainers
— Networking vocational technical training information and exchange of information
— T.A. and training for establishing a sufficient standard of the

training itself and periodical repetitions for maintaining the standard
- T.A. at the training policy planning level
- Train the trainer programs with more follow-up
- How to more effectively get good OJT and industrial training in private agencies
- Rural vocational training which is comprehensive, i.e. for income generation, daily skills and rural infrastructure building and maintenance
- Heavy on practical applications, light on theory, depends on task
- (1) Locally defined needs assessment; (2) long-run planning
- Sharing of curriculum materials, techniques, procedures, in-service, more instructor-to-instructor interchanges
- Training of instructors in use of competency-based materials and methods and how to adapt to local/regional needs
- Improve training infrastructure
- Training of the in-country trainers
- (1) Technology transfer; (2) material adaptation; (3) counterpart establishment
- Training policy-makers and their teacher educators so that they might both establish reasonable policy and implement it with an educational staff
- Curriculum and assessment development
- Developing the economic and training needs as a planned effort
- Train the trainers; they can then train their own workers
- Training of trainers
- (a) Rural vocational training for non-farm occupations; (b) involvement of private sector in training; (c) use of advanced technology for training.
- Combination of group/self-paced training with appropriate training methods and materials
- The most beneficial assistance in the field of training is to provide materials and knowledge to trainers
- Employment generation for youth (especially delinquents)
- Management and evaluation skills
- Training and technical assistance in assessing industry needs in competency-based terms acquiring or developing competency-based instructional materials, assessing competency-based outcomes

ANNEX II
Trends in Government Expenditures and Foreign Aid for Education and Training

A. Share of Central Government Expenditure

In low-income economies (excluding India and China), the percentage of total central government expenditure going to education was a weighted average of 13.2 per cent in 1972, decreasing to a weighted average of 7.6 per cent in 1985. Similar figures for middle-income economies were 14.0 per cent, decreasing to 11.5 per cent; for lower middle-income economies 16.4 per cent, down to 13.8 per cent and for upper middle-income economies 12.3 per cent, down to 10.6 per cent For developing economies by another classification the weighted average percentages were as follows:

Table 1: Percentage of Government Expenditures on the Educational Sector

	1972	1985
	(percentages)	
oil exporters	12.7	13.7
exporters of manufactures	9.6	5.3
highly indebted countries	14.0	9.9
sub-Saharan Africa	13.2	14.5
Totals	13.8	10.4

B. Share of Foreign Aid

World Bank: Between 1963 and 1978, annual lending by the World Bank to the education and training sector increased in absolute terms more than five-fold. As a percentage of all sector lending, it went up from 3 per cent before 1970 to a peak of 8.6

per cent in 1973. It then declined to 4.0 per cent by 1978. There was no clear trend in the proportion of total project costs this borrowed money represented; it fluctuated around a level of about half of the total.

In more recent years, the trends in lending by the World Bank and the IDA to the education sector are shown as follows:

Table 2: World Bank/IDA Lending to the Education Sector

Year	Source	US $ Millions	Percentage of total lending
1985	IBRD	514.9	4.5
	IDA	412.9	13.6
	Total	927.8	6.5
1986	IBRD	577.7	4.4
	IDA	251.5	8.0
	Total	829.2	5.1
1987	IBRD	173.5	1.2
	IDA	266.3	7.6
	Total	439.8	2.5

The World Bank gives information about external education sector aid from OECD and OPEC Members by Level and Type of Education as an average for the years 1981-83 which is attached below (source: *Education in Sub-Saharan Africa,* Washington, 1988, p.150).

Members of DAC: Where 1964=100, in 1967 total assistance from DAC members to developing countries rose to 114, total technical assistance to 140 and total aid to education to 131. In the following decade, there was incomplete reporting to DAC of the figures of total educational experts assigned (by countries selected with the larger numbers):

Table 3: Number of Education Experts, by Country of Origin

Country	1966	1971	1974	1977
Belgium	1957	1579	1487	1255
Germany	806	2825	2753	3038
Japan	17	70	103	151
Netherlands	107	145	367	504
United Kingdom	4354	6426	5068	3846
France	30190	27309	Not Provided	
United States	2328	1511	Not Provided	
Total DAC	42041	102818	Not Provided	

Unfortunately, the 1988 DAC report for the year 1987 does not continue the series given above. It simply reports for these countries the percentage of their total aid going to education, as follows:

Table 4: Percentage of Total Aid to Education

Donor	%
Belgium	28.6
Germany	19.0
Japan	8.1
Netherlands	5.0
United Kingdom	12.8
France	26.5
United States	3.8
Multilateral aid	4.3

This DAC report also offers the following assessment:

> We are apparently spending about one-tenth per cent of our funds for education. A World Bank analysis suggests that historically more funds have gone for higher education over primary education and for capital assistance, overseas

fellowships and technical assistance over support for coherent national strategies. Very little has gone to primary education. If this is an accurate reflection of the facts, then we might at least ask whether or not we are spending our limited funds for education for the wrong things and in the wrong way. (op.cit. p.38)

The figure of 4.3 per cent for multilateral aid indicated above, suggests that a smaller proportion of multilateral than of bilateral aid is going to the education sector. This may be regrettable insofar as developing countries feel the need for assistance in the education field without a marked cultural orientation. This was expressed, for example, by experts on education in developing countries at EDC's Thirtieth Anniversary Symposium and by one or two participants at the recent meeting between UNDP and EDC to discuss EDC's report to UNDP.

UNDP Policy Discussion Papers

Mobilizing Human Potential: The Challenge of Unemployment, by Paul Streeten (1989)

Development and Adjustment: Stabilization, Structural Adjustment and UNDP Policy, by Georges Chapelier and Hamid Tabatabai (1989)

The Impact of Macro-economic Policies on the Rural Poor: Analytical Framework and Indicators, by Jean-Paul Azam, Gerard Chambas, Patrick and Sylviane Guillaumont (1989)

Resolving the Global Debt Crisis, by Morris Miller (1989)

Credit for the Poor: Past Activities and Future Directions for the United Nations Development Programme, by Jeffrey Ashe and Christopher E. Cosslett (1989)

Education and Training in the 1990s: Developing Countries' Needs and Strategies, by Education Development Center (1989)